Keepers of the Way

Keepers of the Way

Copyright © 2016 by Dr. Rob McCord

Published by Plowhand Press, Indianapolis, Indiana

All rights reserved. This book or any portion thereof may not be reproduced or used in any manner whatsoever without the express written permission of the publisher except for the use of brief quotations in a book review or journal.

ISBN 978-0-9984561-0-2

All Scripture quotations, unless otherwise indicated, are taken from the Holy Bible, NEW INTERNATIONAL VERSION®. Copyright © 1973, 1978, 1984, 2011 by Biblica, Inc. All rights reserved worldwide. Used by permission.

Scripture quotations marked (ESV) are taken from The Holy Bible, English Standard Version® (ESV®), copyright © 2001 by Crossway, a publishing ministry of Good News Publishers. Used by permission. All rights reserved.

Scripture quotations marked (Ph) are taken from The New Testament in Modern English by J.B Phillips copyright © 1960, 1972 J. B. Phillips. Administered by The Archbishops' Council of the Church of England. Used by Permission.

Scripture quotations marked (NLT) are taken from the Holy Bible, New Living Translation, copyright © 1996, 2004, 2007 by Tyndale House Foundation. Used by permission of Tyndale House Publishers, Inc., Carol Stream, Illinois 60188. All rights reserved.

Scripture quotations marked (KJV) are taken from the Holy Bible, King James Version.

Quotations are taken from THE MESSAGE. Copyright © by Eugene H. Peterson 1993, 1994, 1995, 1996, 2000, 2001, 2002. Used by permission of Tyndale House Publishers, Inc.

robmccord.org

Cover and book design by Dayshift Art+Design
Cover photo courtesy of Viktor Hanacek

for Elijah and Hope

Does not wisdom call out?
Does not understanding raise her voice?
At the highest point along the way,
where the paths meet, she takes her stand...
"Now then, my children, listen to me;
blessed are those who keep my ways."
[Proverbs 8:1-2,32]

Walk in the ways of the good
and keep to the paths of the righteous.
[Proverbs 2:20]

Contents

Preface	7
1 Be the Change	11
2 Walk the Line	31
3 Always Move Forward	49
4 Stay in the Fight	67
5 Control Yourself	87
6 Defy Expectations	107
7 Focus on Forever	127
8 Belong Together	147
9 Know Better	165
10 Light Up the Place	187
11 Send a Message	209
12 Exclude No One	229
13 Go Ahead	245
Afterword	263
Acknowledgements	269
Endnotes	271

Preface

I'm a Jesus-follower who's called to help others follow Jesus. That's essentially who I am and what I do. This means I'm always searching for ways to follow more fully and help others more effectively. I wrote this book seeking to accomplish both.

You see, in my own discipleship to Jesus I've found I'm drawn to the overarching meaning of it all, the sheer scope of the story and mission, the depth of passion, the strength of purpose. I believe when we lose sight of these our following can quickly become fallow—lifeless, uninspired, ineffectual. So when following Jesus is represented in a way that makes it seem lame, boring, or otherwise less than the epic thing it is, it bothers me greatly. Christians settle and the world suffers. It really is a tragedy beyond words when this happens. I live to help people make sure it doesn't.

What I've attempted to do here is paint a picture of what it means to be a disciple of Jesus *as I see it*, indeed, as I *need* to see it and visualize it if I am to keep to it. I hope you'll find this picture as I do: biblically authentic as well as intellectually stimulating and emotionally compelling. I want to set your faith to a film score, get you in touch with the pathos of it, draw you to it like the magnetic force it is. I believe language—the words we choose and the meaning we assign to them—can be useful to such ends. So can perspective.

My goal is to recast the familiar so you see it in new ways. I want to encourage you to press into the tensions and pressures of living as a Christian in the twenty-first century. If what I've compiled here inspires you to embrace the beautiful truth of Jesus more enthusiastically and wholeheartedly, then my prayers will be answered and my intentions fulfilled.

Dallas Willard, a Christian whose thoughts and teaching I respect deeply, once wrote of Jesus and His modern-day followers: "The ease, lightness, and power of his Way we rarely enjoy, much less see, as the pervasive and enduring quality of our street-level human existence."[1] I observe the truth of this statement in myself and those around me, and you probably do too. We get it, but we don't' *have* it. We appreciate it even as we struggle to keep to it. Far too often we're more obligated than inspired. We trudge when we could run. We hedge instead of risk. And we give in and fit in when it's time to stand up and stand out. We settle, but that's not the Way.

The Way, as our Christward movement was first called, is potent though ancient, unique though seemingly ubiquitous, and vital though often dismissed as irrelevant. It's a good and beautiful Way worth our whole life's devotion and exploration. On it we learn a wisdom and discernment, receive a peace and a purpose, that surpass anything any other way of life can offer. Finding this Way is our greatest discovery; keeping to it our greatest decision. One we make every day. Perhaps our Lord will use this book to help you make that decision once more today. Again, that's my prayer.

This book began as a series of sermons I prepared and preached throughout the autumn of 2015. I had also written a daily devotional to go along with that series, which is now distributed after each chapter. It's been my aim to retain some of the energy and feel of those words spoken from the pulpit while translating them to these written on the page—a process more challenging than I estimated. Whether I've met my aim is for you to decide, but I do sincerely hope the sermons my congregation heard can carry on sufficiently as chapters you'll find engaging.

To be clear, though I've ministered in several countries and count as my co-laborers believers around the world, I should note that I write primarily to American Christians in this book. These are who I pastor, the Christians I know best, and the particular burden of my heart and mind as I prepared these messages. However, I believe any readers outside the United States can appreciate what I'm saying and perhaps will appreciate that I'm saying it to their American siblings in the faith.

As I mentioned, I preached these messages in the fall of 2015 and am writing this preface a year later. What a strange and disconcerting year it's been for us as a nation. Without doubt, our work as the Church is cut out for us. It's more important than ever we keep to the Way of Resistance, Rebellion, and Revolution.

This book is a word to the Church, which began as a word to the church I serve. I'm tremendously grateful for the good people of Outlook Christian Church. Each week they allow me to share with them what I'm learning from God's Word, and in the process they teach me so much. I love them. It's an honor to be one of their pastors.

My prayer for you, dear fellow-follower, is taken from the words of Isaiah the prophet, who saw more clearly than most the Way of the Messiah. In a day not unlike our own, amidst rebuke to a wayward and confused people, he pronounced this blessing:

Whether you turn to the right or to the left, your ears will hear a voice behind you, saying, "This is the way; walk in it." (Isaiah 30:21)

Hands to the plow, eyes on the prize,

McCordsville, Indiana
November 2016

1
BE THE CHANGE

In our modern day it can sometimes feel we're so removed from the times of Scripture, that things just aren't the same today as they were when Jesus taught. So much has changed, it seems. But not everything has changed, and perhaps not as much as we think.

I love change and progress and growth. I enjoy new ideas and appreciate inventiveness. But I also know some things should stay the same, that not all innovation is improvement. Maybe there are some things we can't improve upon, but instead should build our lives upon.

I see today three forces in effect all around us. They are at once both subtle and pervasive. And they are shifting the hearts and minds of many followers of Jesus. We ignore them at our peril.

First, I observe that *because Christianity has been around for a long time now, its familiarity has bred contempt, or at least boredom and cynicism*. We—especially in the West and specifically the United States—have become enamored by the idea that only the latest iteration of something is worthwhile. So much so, we find it hard to fathom that a spirituality taught almost twenty centuries ago need not be, even can't be improved upon. In other words, we ask, "Could the Way of Jesus actually be *the* way, the *best* way, after all this time?"

Secondly, *some Christians in the public sphere are a tragic embarrassment and misrepresentation of our faith, so we hedge our identification with Christianity.* It's unfortunate that the self-described Christians who make headlines are often hateful, spiteful, ignorant, greedy, or duplicitous. In the thesaurus of our current culture, the word "Christian" is too readily—and understandably—associated with the least Christ-like attitudes and behaviors. So we hold back. And instead of rising to reclaim our beautiful designation, we run the risk of allowing it to be drained of its powerful meaning. We find ourselves asking, "Do I really understand what a Christian is? And do I want to be one?"

And thirdly, *as our society is becoming morally and ethically groundless, we are becoming confused by godless but persuasive philosophies and worldviews.* Our modern and post-modern perspectives are becoming untethered from absolute or transcendent truth. Human-centered thinking that doesn't factor God into its equations has become the norm. Some of it can seem pretty convincing, and we begin wondering, "Does Christianity really have the answers for everyone?"

> IN THE THESAURUS OF OUR CURRENT CULTURE, THE WORD "CHRISTIAN" IS TOO READILY ASSOCIATED WITH THE LEAST CHRIST-LIKE ATTRIBUTES.

I've come to believe our confusion about such issues stems from confusion about who we are and where we come from and what we're really all about. In these chapters, I'd like to re-introduce us to some essential realities and re-sound the radical call of discipleship to Jesus Christ...a call to be Keepers of the Way.

THE WAY WE KEEP

This Greek noun we translate as "the way" or "the road" is used repeatedly in the New Testament. How each of us lives our life is likened to a road. Jesus says there are only two. We are all on one or the other.

> Enter through the narrow gate. For wide is the gate and broad is the road that leads to destruction, and many enter through it. But small is the gate and narrow the road that leads to life, and only a few find it. (Matthew 7:13-14)

We do well to remember that Jesus is not saying the way to life is a precarious puzzle or tightrope walk, that a few people make it but most people can't. He's is not *prescribing* the way things should be or are meant to be. He's *describing* the way things are. The way to true life is ignored by most because we want to go our own way or take what we think is the easy way. That's why even today following the path of Jesus hasn't ceased to be a trailblazing decision for each person, each generation.

Later, Jesus makes it clear that He Himself *is* the exit ramp onto this "road that leads to life" and that life with Him *is* this very pathway. He said to Thomas in the hearing of the other disciples, "I am the way and the truth and the life. No one comes to the Father except through me." (John 14:6)

Think of the whole of humanity on a 16-lane highway that sends them careening off a cliff. It takes a broad road to accommodate the many who live ignoring God. This is the geography of the situation: This road leads to death because it leads away from the Giver of life (see Psalm 36:9). But Jesus says there is another road we can choose, though not many do. It's the trail back to our Creator—forged by Jesus, and only Jesus, the Creator Incarnate.

It is this exclusivity—that Jesus is *the* gate to God—which is our faith's most defining and disruptive truth. We are not keepers of *a* way, but *the* Way. Fittingly, "the Way" became the early name of the movement we today call Christianity. And its claim of Jesus' singularity was a serious sticking point for many in the first century. Some things never change.

> **EVEN TODAY, FOLLOWING THE PATH OF JESUS HASN'T CEASED TO BE A TRAILBLAZING DECISION.**

A riot erupted in Ephesus because Paul's claims about Jesus threatened to put some idol-makers out of business. Luke's summary of the situation goes like this: "About that time there arose a great disturbance about the Way." (Acts 19:23) Later, Paul stood before the Roman Governor Felix as his accusers stated, "We have found this man to be a troublemaker." (Acts 24:5) He boldly and clearly answered:

> I do freely admit this: In regard to the Way, which they malign as a dead-end street, I serve and worship the very same God served and

worshiped by all our ancestors and embrace everything written in all our Scriptures. (Acts 24:14 MSG)

The Way was maligned, but held up by Paul as a consistent, ancient path described in the Holy Scriptures, a path worth taking and keeping.

My prayer is that Paul's words could be our words, that you and I could say, "I'm on that Way. I believe what the Scriptures say. I'm following the one true God as revealed in those Scriptures and in the Lord Jesus Christ." Do you know that Way? What can seem like old news to us was new then and is, in reality, eternally new and fresh and available today.

Where does this lead us? What does the Way mean for us today? Christians are pilgrims, non-conformists, and change agents. We always have been. When it comes to our faith, we can become bored or cynical, we can be embarrassed or ashamed, we can get confused or discouraged...but we don't have to. That's not who we are.

> **CHRISTIANS ARE PILGRIMS, NON-CONFORMISTS, AND CHANGE AGENTS. WE ALWAYS HAVE BEEN.**

I'm using some different and—I hope—inspiring terms here to reframe for us how we consider the path of discipleship to Jesus. My intention is that by using such language we can see essential but familiar truths in new ways.

We are pilgrims who join the resistance by humbly living holy lives.

Pilgrims aren't just the folks from the Mayflower we met in elementary school. Pilgrims are people on a spiritual quest, a pilgrimage. They are determined to not simply do what comes naturally—what we call the path of *least* resistance—but to do what comes supernaturally.

We are to be just such pilgrims, empowered by God to choose a path that left to ourselves we could never navigate. Thankfully, we've been promised the traveling companionship of the Holy Spirit living in us as we trek toward "a city whose architect and builder is God." (Hebrews 11:10) We fix our eyes on Jesus and we keep our hand to that plow (Hebrews 12:2 and Luke 9:62). We are on a pilgrimage (Psalm 84:5).

We are resisting the forces that can veer us aside or hold us back or keep us down. The Scriptures speak of *resisting* the devil and *resisting* temptation, of refraining from sin and refusing to live according to our lower nature. Instead, we tend to our character development, pursuing what's right and good, and paying attention to our choices and watching our steps. This is the Resistance. We join it and join in it.

Peter put it like this, "Dear friends, I urge you, as foreigners and exiles, to abstain from sinful desires, which wage war against your soul." (1 Peter 2:11) Pilgrims fight this inner battle. And we must remember it's an inner battle first. We can be far too quick to war against the sin of a godless world, and equally slow to address it in ourselves. That's why before we speak of our rebellion against this world or of a revolution that can change this world, we begin with our own individual resistance.

As pilgrims pursuing holiness, we have an accurate estimation of the danger and tragedy of sin. We don't underestimate it. Additionally, we recalibrate our response to sin wherever we find it. And we often get this wrong. Our first response should not be anger or disgust, but grief. And the first sin to grieve us should be our own. If we haven't at some point in our pilgrimage grieved and wept because of our own sin, we should stop and think about our repentance. If the sin of others living without God or walking away from Him doesn't first grieve us, we must consider our compassion.

> **OUR FIRST RESPONSE TO SIN SHOULD BE GRIEF. AND THE FIRST SIN TO GRIEVE US SHOULD BE OUR OWN.**

For many of us, when faced with the sin of others our first instinct is to shake our fist or wag our finger. But it's our ongoing posture of repentance and compassion that keeps us from being judgmental and condemning. Yes, we know what sin is, and yes, we need to call it for what it is, but when our own spirit of humble repentance guides us, we can do so in constructive—not destructive—ways.

We realize, left to ourselves, we're all flaming in sin of one kind or another. So before we think about all the things we want to change about this world, we soberly consider what God wants to change in us. There's nothing wrong with helping others remove the unhealthy and irritating specks from their eyes, so long as we don't forget that we ourselves are plank-eyed and equally needful (Matthew 7:3-5 and Luke 6:41-42). This is the Resistance, and we are pilgrims who join in it by humbly living holy lives.

WE ARE NON-CONFORMISTS WHO FUEL THE REBELLION BY REORDERING PRIORITIES AND REDEFINING SUCCESS.

This is how it works: we walk in this way of Resistance, concerned first about our own character development, praying to become more like Jesus, transformed by His Spirit. We are pilgrims on a pilgrimage guided by the narrow Way. And as we humbly walk that direction we inevitably find we are going against the flow of prevailing culture, running counter to the way a godless society thinks and behaves. We find ourselves rebelling against the ways of this world, no longer fitting in.

Peter goes on: "Live such good lives among the pagans that, though they accuse you of doing wrong, they may see your good deeds." (1 Peter 2:12) I especially appreciate *The Message* paraphrase of this: "Live an exemplary life among the natives so that your actions will refute their prejudices." We know all too well there are increasing prejudices against Christians in today's world, some of which are understandable. However, our actions as faithful—not perfect, but wholehearted—followers of Jesus can begin to dissolve those prejudices and accusations, casting this Way in a new and healthy light.

> **WE BEGIN TO SEE RIGHT THROUGH WHAT BAITS AND TRAPS OUR SOCIETY AND THE GODLESS PHILOSOPHIES THAT STOKE OUR HUMAN PRIDE.**

That's what I hear Peter saying: Live life well, stay healthy, be true. Don't give in to the pressure to fit in. Let following Jesus have its effect.

What's important to us has changed, so has how we define our worth. We begin to see right through what baits and traps our society and the godless philosophies that stoke our human pride. So many buy into it and fall for it, but we see it for what it is. There's a pattern to this world and we refuse to conform (see Romans 12:2). We see it drifting away from God and we choose the opposite direction. We become rebels with a cause.

WE ARE CHANGE AGENTS WHO ADVANCE THE REVOLUTION BY SACRIFICIALLY LOVING AND SERVING.

Peter concludes his thought by claiming the good lives and deeds of Jesus-followers will convince others to "glorify God on the day he visits us." (1 Peter 2:12) Or, again, as *The Message* puts it: "Then they'll be won over to God's side and be there to join in the celebration when he arrives." What a beautiful picture of the results of the Revolution: hearts changed and ready to party. It's a vision worth giving our lives in sacrificial love and service.

The creative tension between this beautiful *ideal* of the culmination of the Kingdom in human hearts and the crude *real* of the injustices and indignities which surround us everyday drives us onward. It provides the energy for fruitful, genuine change—change we are called to bring, change we alone *can* bring, to this hurting, hurtful world.

We do well to remember Jesus started nothing less than a mission of personal turnaround and global takeover. That is the Revolution: Changed people changing the world. It's revolutionary simply to hope things can change.

And there's plenty of hope. Plenty of opportunities to see people "won over to God's side" to walk in God's Way. Love makes that possible. Love not only in feelings and goosebumps, but also hard work, sacrifice, and service. Love does that.

In 1975, Dan Wooding was a cub newspaper reporter assigned to interview Mother Teresa. Remembering years later that conversation in the slums of Calcutta, Wooding confessed he

> **JESUS STARTED NOTHING LESS THAN A REVOLUTION OF PERSONAL TURNAROUND AND GLOBAL TAKEOVER.**

was surprised to hear Mother Teresa express her pity for the "poverty-stricken West." She observed, "The spiritual poverty of the Western World is much greater than the physical poverty of our people."[1] Over her years, this is a diagnosis she often shared:

There are many in the world who are dying for a piece of bread but there are many more dying for a little love. The poverty in the West is a different kind of poverty—it is not only a poverty of loneliness but also of spirituality. There's a hunger for love, as there is a hunger for God.[2]

I believe her words are no less true today. Love is the key. We "go into all the world" because "God so loved the world" (Mark 16:15 and John 3:16).

It can be easy to think that this revolution should be enacted through new laws on our books or new limits on our media or new leaders in our institutions. Any and all of these may be useful or wise at given times and places, but they are at best the by-products of the real Revolution. It's new hearts that are the seat of true change. It's only Christ's spiritual transformation of the individual that yields the reformation of the world.

Resistance, rebellion, revolution...

What we are describing is essentially the path of discipleship. It starts with our own internal resistance, our own inner concern for holiness and spiritual maturity, for our own character development, for our ability to say yes to what's good and no to what's not. This puts us in a position of cultural rebellion. We're no longer at home in this world, no longer entirely comfortable with everything this world says is important or true. And then from that humble posture we turn to change the world with love.

> **LOVE IS THE KEY. WE "GO INTO ALL THE WORLD" BECAUSE "GOD SO LOVED THE WORLD."**

Resistance, rebellion, revolution...these terms resonate with me and I hope they will with you as well. They are recurring themes not only in Scripture but in history.

Dietrich Bonhoeffer was a young pastor and professor who ultimately gave his life seeking to overthrow Nazi Germany. He believed his opposition was the natural embodiment of his Christian convictions. He worked tirelessly to call his fellow Christians to clarify their thinking and get their faith into meaningful action. This certainly describes my goal in writing this book. He wrote these words from prison, powerful then and relevant for us today:

We have been silent witnesses of evil deeds; we have been drenched by many storms; we have learnt the arts of equivocation and pretence; experience has made us suspicious of others and kept us from being truthful and open; intolerable conflicts have worn us down and even made us cynical. Are we still of any use?

I can't help but feel there may be not a small number of Christians who feel much like this today.

The headlines we read about the atrocities of abortion, the abuses of power, the attacks of terror...we have been (perhaps silent?) "witnesses of evil deeds." We've endured many things that have perhaps made us suspicious and kept us from being transparent about our faith. Conflicts have "worn us down." And we look around and ask ourselves today: "Are we still of any use?" This world seems to be going on without us. But hear Bonhoeffer's answer:

What we shall need is not geniuses, or cynics, or misanthropes, or clever tacticians, but plain, honest, and straightforward men. Will our inward power of resistance be strong enough, and our honesty with ourselves remorseless enough, for us to find our way back to simplicity and straightforwardness?[3]

Do you hear what he's saying here? We don't need clever innovations or new answers. We need simplicity and straightforwardness. What a beautiful description of the Way: simple and straight and not difficult to understand.

Can we find "our inward power of resistance" so we can "find our way back?" Can we be keepers of the Way, humble and wholehearted men and women who simply and honestly live out our faith, this beautiful way to live?

> **WE DON'T NEED CLEVER INNOVATIONS OR NEW ANSWERS. WE NEED SIMPLICITY AND STRAIGHTFORWARDNESS.**

Honestly, we must. For the sake of our own souls and—if it doesn't sound overdramatic—for the sake of the world. Some say we live in "Bonhoeffer moments" today. I'm more than inclined to agree.

The way forward is back at the beginning.

Let's find our way back, back to the beginning, back to the birth of the Church, the conception of our cause, the DNA of the Way. Remember the scene: Thousands of people are in Jerusalem, the Holy Spirit has been poured out onto and into this initial gathering of believers, and Peter is preaching, explaining who Jesus is, what's He's done, and how His Spirit empowers. He draws from their Jewish scripture, he refers to the recent events of the cross and the empty tomb, and *they are getting it*. "They were cut to the heart and said to Peter and the other apostles, 'Brothers, what shall we do?'" (Acts 2:37)

You see, this is not a truth to which I can passively listen and say, "Maybe later." Once it's explained, I realize there is a God, He is real, He knows me, and I've been living apart from Him. That was foolish. I have a decision to make now. What am I going to do about this new reality, this new truth that has become clear to me? Hear Peter's answer, these words of resistance, rebellion, revolution (for that is what they are): "Repent and be baptized, every one of you, in the name of Jesus Christ for the forgiveness of your sins. And you will receive the gift of the Holy Spirit." (Acts 2:38)

> **MANY CENTURIES LATER AND PERHAPS "FAR OFF," THE CALL IS NO LESS CLEAR AND THE PROMISE IS NO LESS REAL.**

There's the Resistance. This verb, repent (*metanoeō*, from the same root as *metamorphosis*), is all about changing our mind and our ways out of remorse from our sins. We do this when we approach the reality of our separation from God, our role and responsibility in it, and turn from it. Sorrow, turning, change...it's all packed into this single word. You hear that message and you accept it as true, and receive the salvation it preaches as the gift it is.

Peter continued, "The promise is for you and your children and for all who are far off—for all whom the Lord our God will call." (Acts 2:39) That's you and me. Many centuries later and perhaps "far off," the call is no less clear and the promise is no less real. Make this story your story. If you're already a Jesus-follower, I encourage you to live out your baptism. It's not simply something that happened to us sometime in the past, it's something that's happening in us every day. The saying goodbye to the old and hello to the new, the dying to self and sin, the acceptance of new life, the posture of repentance...none of this becomes an iota less relevant after your baptism. That's the Resistance.

We then read that with many other words Peter warned them and pleaded with them, "Save yourselves from this corrupt generation." (Acts 2:40) These are words of our Rebellion. Peter's plea is the plea of this book. Leave the broad road. Find and take the Way. Keep to it.

When we do, it's revolutionary. "Those who accepted his message were baptized, and about three thousand were added to their number that day." (Acts 2:41) And the Church hasn't looked back. The Revolution had begun. People keep being added to that number. Maybe you. Definitely—thank God—me, too.

Listen, I get it.

Maybe you've gotten bored with this ancient faith and it's lost its beauty for you. You're wondering if it's still relevant.

Maybe you've distanced yourself because some give our cause a bad name. You're wondering where you fit.

Maybe you've gotten confused or dizzied or just exhausted by what can seem like so many competing philosophies. You're wondering what's right.

Let's find the Way together. Because it's still there and it's still so good. It's as beautiful and relevant and truthful as ever. It's as needed and healthy and useful as ever. We can keep it and keep to it and show it to the world. Jesus doesn't change because He can't be improved upon (see Hebrews 13:8). He's as compelling and brilliant as ever. Let's build our lives on His truth and get reacquainted with this Way of life. It's the best.

> ENTER THROUGH THE NARROW GATE. FOR
> WIDE IS THE GATE AND BROAD IS THE ROAD
> THAT LEADS TO DESTRUCTION, AND MANY
> ENTER THROUGH IT. BUT SMALL IS THE GATE
> AND NARROW THE ROAD THAT LEADS TO LIFE,
> AND ONLY A FEW FIND IT.
> [MATTHEW 7:13-14]

Ever happily head down the highway only to realize at some point you missed your exit and aren't getting to where you need to be? It's frustrating to say the least. When the same kind of mistake is made on the road of life, it's downright fatal. We must choose—and choose wisely—the way we take.

Navigating isn't always easy. Charting a course through life on our own is definitely not easy. But Jesus says His Way is imminently available, though often overlooked. Take it. And resolve to not wander from it. Ask yourself: How adhered am I to the narrow Way? How easily do I drift from it?

> **HOW EACH OF US LIVES OUR LIVES IS LIKE A ROAD EACH OF US WALKS. JESUS SAYS THERE ARE ONLY TWO.**

---WE PRAY---

"Jesus, I praise You for providing the road that leads to life."

I AM THE WAY AND THE TRUTH AND THE LIFE. NO ONE COMES TO THE FATHER EXCEPT THROUGH ME.
[JOHN 14:6]

It's popular today to believe that all roads lead to God, that any sincere seeker can find God any way they choose. It's a comfortable but nonsensical thought. If I want to reach you by phone, not just any set of digits I choose will work—no matter how sincerely I dial them. But if you've given me your number, that's a different situation altogether. And I'd be a fool to ignore it.

This is exactly analogous to our pursuit of the divine. Essentially, God has given us His number in Jesus. But we humans want to make up our own.

Exclusivity sometimes simply reflects reality. Think about it: If God is anything more than an amorphous idea or concept, doesn't it make sense that we can't connect with Him just any way we choose, but instead should learn the Way He provides? What keeps us and others from doing this?

> **NOTHING'S MORE ESSENTIAL TO OUR WELLBEING THAN REUNION WITH OUR MAKER. JESUS PROVIDES THE WAY.**

---WE PRAY---

"Father, I want more than anything to come to You through the grace of Jesus"

LET US THROW OFF EVERYTHING THAT HINDERS
AND THE SIN THAT SO EASILY ENTANGLES.
AND LET US RUN WITH PERSEVERANCE THE RACE
MARKED OUT FOR US, FIXING OUR EYES ON JESUS,
THE PIONEER AND PERFECTER OF FAITH.
[HEBREWS 12:1-2]

So often we don't see our own handicaps. We are blind to our blind spots. We need perspective. By ourselves, using only our selves as a measure of health and wholeness, we will not run well for long, but will sooner or later run our lives into the ditch. That sounds harsh, but it's just our human lot.

We must look to the One who sees us perfectly, who has blazed the trail for us, and who wants very much for us to live victoriously. Only He can show us what we most need to know: the hindrances and entanglements we don't realize are ruining us. And only He can free us from them. Ask Him: What must I throw away so I can run the race You've marked out for me?

> **WE MUST GLADLY GET RID OF ALL THAT TRIPS US UP AND WEIGHS US DOWN. NONE OF IT IS WORTH LOSING OUR FOCUS.**

—— WE PRAY ——

"Jesus, I fix my eyes on You who goes before me and makes me whole."

> DEAR FRIENDS, I URGE YOU, AS FOREIGNERS
> AND EXILES, TO ABSTAIN FROM SINFUL DESIRES,
> WHICH WAGE WAR AGAINST YOUR SOUL.
> [1 PETER 2:11]

When we're far from home, in a foreign land, we pay special attention to what's happening around us. We give extra thought to what we eat, where we go, how we treat others. This is true in peacetime; it's many times more true when war's been declared. Peter is reminding us there's a war on. It's a war for our souls.

It's not a war with others or with our culture, but a spiritual war, a war within. We needn't be militant, but a wartime mentality can serve us well. We must be alert and aware. Give it some thought: How long can I go seemingly forgetting I am indeed in a fight for my spiritual life?

> **THE INTERNAL BATTLES WE FIGHT HAVE ETERNAL CONSEQUENCES AND REMIND US THIS WORLD ISN'T OUR HOME.**

---WE PRAY---

"Lord, strengthen me for battle against the dark forces of this foreign world."

> LIVE SUCH GOOD LIVES AMONG THE PAGANS THAT,
> THOUGH THEY ACCUSE YOU OF DOING WRONG,
> THEY MAY SEE YOUR GOOD DEEDS AND
> GLORIFY GOD ON THE DAY HE VISITS US.
> [1 PETER 2:12]

"I'll believe it when I see it," is the skeptic's response to a claim or promise. And when it comes to Christianity, our neighbors have reason to be skeptical. The ugly words and hateful conduct of a few have tarnished the reputation of our precious faith. We must counter their example with a better, truer one that burnishes God's beauty in the eyes of those who are apart from Him.

Actions really do speak more loudly than words, and our "good deeds" can speak volumes to a dubious and disparaging world. Consider: Is God's goodness obvious enough in my behavior and lifestyle to convince others of His reality?

> **ARGUMENTS ABOUT IDEAS AND BELIEFS ARE INEVITABLE, BUT RESULTS BORNE IN VIRTUOUS ACTION ARE IRREFUTABLE.**

---WE PRAY---

"God, may others glorify You because of the goodness You've grown in me."

SAVE YOURSELVES FROM THIS CORRUPT GENERATION.
[ACTS 2:40]

It's been said that if a frog is placed in a kettleful of water and then that kettle is heated gradually, just a degree at a time, the frog won't bother trying to escape and will eventually be boiled to death. This is usually shared as a cautionary tale warning of the risks of not paying attention to the detrimental or dangerous changes happening around us. Acclimation—gradual degrees of acceptance—to a degrading culture can lead to our downfall. It sounds dramatic, but it's painfully accurate.

Most of our rebelling against this degradation lies in realizing it's occurring and that we needn't stay in the kettle. Ask God: Have I gotten used to something that could ruin me? What am I accepting that I should be rejecting?

> **WE MUST FIND THE WAY OUT OF A SYSTEM AND SOCIETY THAT PROUDLY IGNORES GOD AND ULTIMATELY GOES NOWHERE.**

---WE PRAY---

"Spirit, give me the power to escape the corruption of a godless world."

JOIN THE RESISTANCE

BE ALERT AND OF SOBER MIND
[1 PETER 5:8]

 JOIN THE RESISTANCE

2
WALK THE LINE

I have always loved Johnny Cash's song, *I Walk the Line*. Recorded in 1956, it was one of his earliest hits, and it speaks to me on multiple levels. In this Mr. Cash and I have something in common.

Cash grew up loving gospel music, but Sam Phillips, the owner of Sun Records, insisted there was no market for it. In fact, when he first heard *I Walk the Line*, Phillips didn't like the tempo. Cash wanted the song to be a ballad.

But Phillips asked Cash at the end of the recording session to do one up-tempo version of the song, just for fun. He reluctantly agreed. Soon after, Cash was shocked to hear the up-tempo version of *I Walk the Line* on the radio. Phillips had sneakily pressed that last recording onto vinyl and released it.

But Johnny couldn't object too much. The song became a hit.

Interestingly, Cash got the last laugh over Sam Phillips. While Phillips didn't publish Cash's preferred version of *I Walk the Line*, Johnny figured out a way to smuggle a gospel song past the record producer.

You see, Cash sometimes spoke of a second meaning to *I Walk the Line*. He missed singing gospel music, so he wrote *I Walk the Line* as an expression of spiritual as well as marital fidelity. During an interview just months before his death, he smiled and told and interviewer, "Sam never knew it, but *I Walk the Line* was my first gospel hit."[1]

As we begin part one of this journey together, we're learning about what it means to join the Resistance, to change the world by first allowing ourselves to be changed, letting Christ form our character, and dedicating ourselves to "walk the line." We are resonating with the ancient Way of Christ—a movement initially called "The Way"—and pledging ourselves to keeping this Way.

The Resistance begins with our own individual refusal to take sin lightly and our commitment to quit choosing *the path of least resistance*, but instead choose the path of humility, vigilance, and holiness. **Our first work of the Resistance is in ourselves, guarding our hearts and living out our baptisms.**

IN HUMILITY, WE UNDERSTAND WE SHOULDN'T COMPLETELY TRUST OURSELVES.

Maybe you've never heard it put that way before, or maybe this is a lesson life has already taught you. It runs counter to a lot of what we hear these days. But taking our faith in Christ seriously means taking seriously the sin inside us and our potential to hurt ourselves and others.

Paul put it like this to his young protégée, Timothy: "Here is a trustworthy saying that deserves full acceptance: Christ Jesus came into the world to save sinners—of whom I am the worst." (1 Timothy 1:15) Please realize, Paul is not condemning himself. This is the same man who wrote in Romans 8:1, "There is now no condemnation for those who are in Christ Jesus." He's not being unnecessarily hard on himself; he's humbly assessing himself. He's confronting the brutal facts and making a statement he asserts we would all do well to accept and adopt for ourselves. In fact, I can see how this would be a very healthy confession to make regularly, to hear ourselves say out loud, "Christ Jesus came into the world to save sinners—of whom I am the worst."

> **OUR FIRST WORK OF THE RESISTANCE IS IN OURSELVES, GUARDING OUR HEARTS AND LIVING OUT OUR BAPTISMS.**

German writer, philosopher, and scientist Johann Wolfgang von Goethe once wrote, "I have never heard of a sin being committed without knowing full well that I had the seed of it within myself."[2] That's a humble, realistic assessment of our own humanness. Watch the news, scroll the headlines, listen to the heartbreaking stories of people hurting and exploiting others. And then say and mean the old but profound words, "There, but for the grace of

God, go I." When we can see this for the truth it is, we are tasting true humility and joining the Resistance.

Know this: The first step in any form of false teaching that steers us from the Way almost always includes the minimization of sin. We downplay this to our downfall. As keepers of the Way in a changing world, we may—and should—find it upsetting when the world calls right what we see God calling wrong. But we also must get upset when *we* begin to call *our* wrong as—not right, (most of us wouldn't go that far), but something more insidious—no big deal. How deeply does it trouble us when we convince ourselves that what God commands is—at least for us on some days—merely what He recommends? We're easy on ourselves while we're hard on the world, and we're losing credibility day by day.

> **WE'RE EASY ON OURSELVES WHILE WE'RE HARD ON THE WORLD, AND WE'RE LOSING CREDIBILITY EVERYDAY.**

Keepers of the Way realize the only thing about us worth magnifying is our redemption. "May I never boast except in the cross of our Lord Jesus Christ," Paul wrote in humble self-awareness, "through which the world has been crucified to me, and I to the world." (Galatians 6:14) We glory in our salvation and in how sorely we need it. We are, in and of ourselves, no better than any other person on the planet. And more than that, left to ourselves we're not always good for ourselves. We need God and we know it. We were built to need God and not to rely on ourselves without Him.

But this concept of self-doubt, of not completely trusting ourselves, is counter to our culture's thinking. David Brooks is a journalist and op-ed writer for *The New York Times*, and in his book, *The Road to Character*, he makes this insightful observation:

> As I looked around the popular culture I kept finding the same messages everywhere: You are special. Trust yourself. Be true to yourself. ...Commencement speeches are larded with the same clichés: Follow your passion. Don't accept limits. Chart your own course. You have a responsibility to do great things because you are so great. This is the gospel of self-trust.[3]

"The gospel of self-trust"...what a telling way to put it. His book is not about Christianity or even faith per se, but I believe Brooks is making an observation helpful to us. This message of self-trust sounds great, and we hear it everywhere.

As television personality Ellen DeGeneres put it in a 2009 commencement address, "My advice to you is to be true to yourself and everything will be fine."

Celebrity chef Mario Batali advised graduates to follow "your own truth, expressed consistently by you."

Journalist Anna Quindlen urged another audience to have the courage to "honor your character, your intellect, your inclinations, and, yes, your soul by listening to its clean clear voice."

In her mega-selling book *Eat, Pray, Love*, Elizabeth Gilbert wrote that God manifests himself through "my own voice from within my own self. ...God dwells within you as you yourself, exactly the way you are."[4] (Can I just say that the last thing I need is God to be me, or to be like me? That's the opposite of what I need.)

I don't share any of this to bash these folks personally, but only to illustrate how pervasive and persuasive this line of thinking is. The things of which we can convince ourselves sound wonderful, but in the end aren't helpful. Instead, we must realize we shouldn't completely trust ourselves because we're fallen and fragile and clearly broken. The gospel of self-trust runs counter to the Gospel of Jesus.

That gospel of grace and wisdom also reveals to me my internal confusion and duplicity. My soul doesn't have a "clean clear voice." My "truth" isn't always true, always accurate. *Exactly the way I am* is exactly what needs to change. I am, or at least too often can be, my own worst enemy. Maybe you can relate. Thankfully, we have a friend in Jesus. When encountering the growing ministry of Jesus, John the baptizer made a statement that can be a lifetime prayer for us all: "He must become greater, I must become less." (John 3:30) In wise humility we understand: I don't need more of me, but more of Him.

> **WE REALIZE WE SHOULDN'T COMPLETELY TRUST OURSELVES BECAUSE WE'RE FALLEN AND FRAGILE AND CLEARLY BROKEN.**

With vigilance, we pay close attention to our character.

We understand what's at stake. When we minimize the meaning of sin we're underestimating the effect of our sin and the real dangers of leaving the Way. It's a tragic miscalculation, which also includes discounting the promise of Jesus to transform our character. It's a powerful promise of change and growth—in one sense sudden, in another gradual—if we choose to cooperate.

So when it comes to walking the line and keeping the Way, this means we pay attention. We are vigilant.

But we mustn't misunderstand: It's not a tightrope we're walking, a test we're bound to fail. Our salvation, our life in Christ, is not a precarious thing resting on a razor's edge or hanging by a thread, the whole thing lost with any misstep. However, it is also not a path without its dangers and distractions. So we watch our step. There's a lot at stake.

Johnny Cash sang it this way: "I keep a close watch on this heart of mine. I keep my eyes wide open all the time."

> **DECISIONS SET DIRECTION IN OUR LIVES. THEIR EFFECTS FOLLOW AN EXPONENTIAL, NOT A LINEAR, COURSE.**

And Proverbs puts it like this: "Above all else, guard your heart, for everything you do flows from it." (4:23) and later reminds us: "For your ways are in full view of the Lord, and he examines all your paths." (5:21)

C.S. Lewis in *Mere Christianity* described the same dynamic: "Good and evil both increase at compound interest. That is why the little decisions you and I make every day are of such infinite importance." Decisions set direction in our lives. Their effects follow an exponential, not a linear, course. Our character today is the culmination of our choices so far. And our character tomorrow is being formed by our choices today. Lewis goes on...

> The smallest good act today is the capture of a strategic point from which, a few months later, you may be able to go on to victories you never dreamed of. An apparently trivial indulgence in lust or anger today is the loss of a ridge or railway line or bridgehead from which the enemy may launch an attack otherwise impossible.[5]

The little decisions we make each day set us in one direction or another, keeping us on the Way or veering us—even if ever so slightly—off the Way. In other words, there are no little decisions. Taking the clickbait in our social media feed for a few seconds of indulgence may seem to be no big deal. Letting the driver who hacks us off during our morning commute keep us in a state of anger all day is letting something small lead to something not as small. We give up a little bit of room in our hearts, a bit of ground in the battlefield of our minds, and it tilts the balance of power in our souls, allowing a corner of real estate to be built upon by less than constructive forces. Decisions set direction. Everything has momentum. It's the physics of faith.

We know our daily choices can have eternal consequences. So we choose every day to make our way the Way of Jesus. It's a daily choice. Paul said to Titus that "Jesus Christ...gave himself for us to redeem us from all wickedness and to purify for himself a people that are his very own, eager to do what is good." (Titus 2:13-14) What a great description of what it means to be a Jesus-follower, a keeper of the Way. We've been redeemed by Jesus and now we're no longer held hostage by all the wickedness inside and outside us that distracts and harms our souls. But instead we can be purified people, never completely perfect, but on our way, every day, to becoming people "eager to do what is good."

> **WE MUST RESET THIS WORD *HOLINESS* IN OUR VOCABULARY AS SOMETHING POSSIBLE AND WORTHY OF OUR PURSUIT.**

THROUGH HOLINESS, WE SEE THE PRECIOUSNESS AND BEAUTY OF LIFE WELL LIVED.

We should, I think, refresh for ourselves this word *holiness*, and take away from it the "holier than thou" connotation it sometimes carries. We must reset it again in our vocabulary as something worthy of our pursuit and, biblically speaking, something possible and to be expected in the life of faith. We are set apart by God and we live for Him—never flawless, but wholehearted and holy, always growing and by God's Spirit getting better at choosing what is right and saying no to the wrong. That is absolutely possible. It must be, if we are to become people who are "eager to do what is good." That's a great description of living with and in holiness, thinking of it not simply as moral perfection but rightly as continuous improvement. Doing right, yes, but also doing good.

This is what Paul's talking about in Romans where, again, the blessing of baptism captures the core of this truth so well. "We were therefore buried with him through baptism into death in order that, just as Christ was raised from the dead through the glory of the Father, we too may live a new life." (Romans 6:4) Just as Jesus was "buried" in that tomb—and didn't stay there long—so we and our old self and our former life are buried—dead and gone—under the water in baptism. And just as Jesus was raised from death and from that tomb so He raises us from those waters and our old self and our former life to live a new life. "New life." I love the sound of that. It's the promise of the Gospel and the point of holiness.

In such newness and holiness, we see the preciousness and beauty of a life lived well by following Jesus. As we

> **IT'S NOT A STRINGENT DUTY, BUT A JOYFUL FOLLOWING, A CONSCIOUS CHOOSING OF WHAT'S RIGHT AND GOOD.**

encounter Jesus, we see the contrast of our old life and decide to turn around and head a new direction, His direction. So we walk the line, keep to the Way, because it's so good. It's not an agonizing trudging. The wind of the Spirit is at our backs and the energy of a renewed heart brings spring to our step. It's not a stringent duty, but a joyful following, a conscious choosing of what's right and good. Before, we couldn't do it; now, we can. "I've *got* to," we used to tell ourselves. Now we happily realize, "I *get* to." We get to live life as God intended it. We were powerless to do that without Him, now this Way is available to us. Now we see it as the resplendent thing it is, purchased by Jesus, paved by His sacrificial love, and offered to us. This is the perspective of the Resistance.

But let's be honest, this perspective isn't always clear to us. There's a fog of false thinking that obscures our view. Its theme goes like this: Because of grace, we needn't concern ourselves much with ethical living or integrity of character. Discerning what's right and what's not is futile. All is forgiven. "God is love" and "Judge not" are the favorite scriptural snippets of those who slip into this way of thinking, one certainly finding popularity today.

Does grace give us permission to ignore what the Grace-giver says about life and how to live it? Of course not. It makes no sense when it's put that way. But such easy-believism can be tempting to us all. As A.W. Tozer once observed several decades ago, it is really a heretical lie:

> A notable heresy has come into being throughout evangelical Christian circles—the widely accepted concept that we humans can choose to accept Christ only because we need him as Savior and that we have the right to postpone our obedience to him as Lord as long as we want to![6]

Grace frees us *to* obey Jesus, not *from* obeying Him. He's not laying on us how we *should* live, but laying out for us how *to* live—and live well. We keep to the Way not to earn His favor but to learn His wisdom. As Dallas Willard unforgettably put it,

> Grace is opposed to earning, not to effort. ...The true saint burns grace like a 747 burns fuel on takeoff. Become the kind of person who routinely does what Jesus did and said. You will consume much more grace by leading a holy life than you will by sinning.[7]

Instead of seeing grace as only that which erases our guilt, we must see it more fully as that which empowers our holiness.

As keepers of the Way we live out our baptisms and cut through this cloud of confused theology. We're learning what repentance means. It's not feeling sorry yet continuing to choose our own way. The Bible calls that mere worldly sorrow that leads to death. Godly sorrow leads to repentance (2 Corinthians 7:10). And repentance leads to life (Acts 11:18). There is a right and wrong. Finding the right and rejecting the wrong is a beautiful thing, a vital step toward thriving as human beings, and the very definition of joining the Resistance and walking the line.

> **WE MUST SEE GRACE NOT ONLY AS ERASING OUR GUILT, BUT EMPOWERING OUR HOLINESS.**

Tragically, the beauty of the Way of repentance isn't appreciated by all. That's always been true. This proverb captures the reality of the situation well:

The stupid ridicule right and wrong, but a moral life is a favored life. (Proverbs 14:9 MSG)
Fools mock at making amends for sin, but goodwill is found among the upright. (NIV)
Fools laugh at sin, but the favor of God is among the faithful. (NLV)

These are not laughing matters. I believe this is not only a description of our world today, but the cause of an incalculable amount of suffering. It is also the epitome of human pride. Those of us who still perceive there's a right and a wrong and the Bible has something to say about that are considered idiots, mocked for taking sin seriously. "What an outdated and old-fashioned concept," some might say. "Get with the times. It's the twenty-first century."

But such modernized morality is proven foolish by its fruit. The Way of Jesus, though ancient, is brilliant. It is the way to life, and we've made it our way of life.

In this chapter discussing humility and vigilance and holiness, I do not want any reader to walk away with the impression I am saying the Christian life is easy. Or that it's about being squeaky-clean. Or that's it's easy to be squeaky-clean. That's why I'm using the term *resistance*. It is a struggle. It is ongoing. It recognizes there's a gravitational pull that runs counter to the Way, but we've been empowered to overcome that, to break out of its orbit, and follow Jesus. It is only in such following, this steady keeping of our eyes on Jesus, that humility, vigilance, and holiness can grow in us.

Johnny Cash was a Christian. And like all of us, he sometimes had a very hard time walking the line. Becoming addicted to drugs and becoming a mostly absent husband and father, he lost his first marriage and at points lost his way. But he never gave up trying to "walk the line." He reconciled with his children. And he kept coming back to God, over and over, even in his darkest days.

Whatever your story has contained, as you're reading this page please know: It's not over. There are new chapters to be written in your story, and God has a pen in His hand ready to write if you give Him room.

Johnny Cash, a fellow Waykeeper, gave us in *I Walk the Line* another way of singing *I Have Decided to Follow Jesus*. And like him, I hope you've decided to follow Jesus, no matter what your journey has been so far.

What we've covered in this chapter is poignantly expressed in Cash's famous song...

In humility, "I keep a close watch on this heart of mine."

With vigilance, "I keep my eyes wide open all the time."

Through holiness (harkening back to an old hymn), "I keep the ends out for the tie the binds."

Jesus, "because You're mine, I walk the line."

> JESUS CHRIST...GAVE HIMSELF FOR US TO REDEEM US
> FROM ALL WICKEDNESS AND TO PURIFY FOR HIMSELF
> A PEOPLE THAT ARE HIS VERY OWN,
> EAGER TO DO WHAT IS GOOD.
> [TITUS 2:13-14]

This movement has been initiated by Jesus. It is His desire to redeem and purify us so we can finally live the lives we were intended to live...healthy, whole lives connected to our Creator and making a difference in this world.

The love of Christ achieved our redemption. What does our love for Christ achieve? What good is His goodness doing in and through us? Ask yourself: What am I eager to do? And of those things, how many of them are good and good for me and others?

> **THROUGH FAITH IN CHRIST WE BECOME HIS PEOPLE, RESCUED BY HIM AND MADE INTO HIS FORCE FOR GOOD.**

─── WE PRAY ───

"Jesus, thank You for saving me and calling me to follow You."

HERE IS A TRUSTWORTHY SAYING THAT DESERVES FULL ACCEPTANCE: CHRIST JESUS CAME INTO THE WORLD TO SAVE SINNERS—OF WHOM I AM THE WORST.
[1 TIMOTHY 1:15]

At first, Paul's admission here may seem extreme, but the point he's making is essential for all of us. Joining the Resistance means recognizing that no matter what, no one needs the Good News of Jesus more than we do. Not only does this keep us humble (which is so important), it also keeps us reliant upon Jesus (which is even more important).

Reflect on this: How easy is it for me to begin to forget just what a mess I'd be without the salvation and love of Jesus?

> **WE UNDERSTAND THE GOSPEL BEST WHEN WE NEVER LOSE SIGHT OF JUST HOW MUCH WE NEED ITS POWER EVERY DAY.**

---WE PRAY---

"Lord, keep me humble and always aware of just how much I need You."

> WE WERE THEREFORE BURIED WITH HIM
> THROUGH BAPTISM INTO DEATH IN ORDER THAT,
> JUST AS CHRIST WAS RAISED FROM THE DEAD
> THROUGH THE GLORY OF THE FATHER,
> WE TOO MAY LIVE A NEW LIFE.
> [ROMANS 6:4]

While we must never forget we're sinners saved by grace, it's equally important we see that in Christ we are now empowered to become so much more than that. We can now live new lives that reflect God's goodness. Incredible! This is encapsulated in our baptism—our immersion into the death and resurrection of Jesus—which is meant to be a pattern for our new lives.

Consider: How can the truth and decision conveyed in my baptism affect how I live today?

> **OUR BAPTISM ISN'T JUST SOMETHING THAT HAPPENS ONCE; IT'S SOMETHING WE LIVE OUT EVERY DAY.**

---WE PRAY---

"Christ, I want to live each day in the reality of my baptism...new in You."

IN THE SAME WAY, COUNT YOURSELVES DEAD TO SIN BUT ALIVE TO GOD IN CHRIST JESUS.
[ROMANS 6:11]

The death we speak about when it comes to our baptized life is a death to our old self, wrapped in selfishness, small thinking, and sin. This means as we encounter sin and temptation we no longer approach them as we used to. And they no longer have the effect on us they used to, either.

The Resistance is about walking above the gravitational pull of our lower natures, about refusing to be moved by what used to attract us, refusing to chase what used to bait us. That's no longer who we are.

Examine yourself: Have I found this to be true in my life? How can I make this more real in my everyday?

> **AS WE LIVE OUR NEW LIFE IN CHRIST, WE FIND OURSELVES INCREASINGLY NUMBED TO THE ALLURE OF SIN.**

———WE PRAY———

"Help me, Jesus, to count myself dead to sin and alive in You."

> MAY I NEVER BOAST EXCEPT IN THE CROSS OF
> OUR LORD JESUS CHRIST, THROUGH WHICH
> THE WORLD HAS BEEN CRUCIFIED TO ME,
> AND I TO THE WORLD.
> [GALATIANS 6:14]

This new life not only frees us from the slavery of sin, it alters our understanding of this world. Jesus' sacrifice on the cross actually happened, in real time and at a real place. And it changed history—our history and world history. It is this reality that nourishes our resistance. We see this world and our place in it in a whole new way.

Chew on this: If my life were being written as a novel or screenplay, how would my encounter with the cross of Christ read among the other significant plot points and even plot twists?

> **THE CROSS OF CHRIST IS THE RESOUNDING THEME AND PIVOTAL POWER OF HIS DISCIPLES' DAILY LIVES.**

―― WE PRAY ――

"Lord, may I only boast about Your grace to me and my gratitude for You."

> SINCE EVERYTHING WILL BE DESTROYED IN THIS WAY,
> WHAT KIND OF PEOPLE OUGHT YOU TO BE?
> YOU OUGHT TO LIVE HOLY AND GODLY LIVES
> AS YOU LOOK FORWARD TO THE DAY OF GOD
> AND SPEED ITS COMING.
> [2 PETER 3:11-12]

We are living within the story of God, which has a powerful and decisive ending. On that day it will be all about Him and His holy plan. Keeping up our Resistance means keeping our eyes on that day and desiring to be found following Him.

This reality check should sharpen our decisions about life and how to live it. As a poem by missionary C.T. Studd profoundly reminds us, "Only one life, 'twill soon be past. Only what's done for Christ will last." Ponder this: What can I do today that may last forever?

> **OUR EARTHLY LIVES ARE TEMPORARY, BUT OUR CHOICES AND ACTIONS HAVE ETERNAL CONSEQUENCES.**

---WE PRAY---

"God, make me an accelerator of Your arrival."

3
Always Move Forward

On spring break several years ago, our family enjoyed a simple getaway at an inn within one of our state parks. The kids and I spent more than a little time in the inn's game room. There was ping-pong, air hockey, and a few little arcade games, including one of those "crane" games, for lack of another term. You know the kind; it's full of stuffed animals and toys and has a crane or claw at the top that can be maneuvered and lowered in hopes of snatching a prize. My name for it is *the dreamcrusher*. Let me tell you why.

My daughter Hope was eight years old, and she loved these things. Usually, I'd give her the same speech about how they're a complete waste. But we were on vacation, and I spared her the blessing of my logic just this once. "Here's 50 cents, sweetheart. Give it a try." Of course, no such luck.

We go on playing ping-pong just a couple feet away from the dreamcrusher. Then an employee arrives and opens each of the games to do a little maintenance, collect proceeds from the dashed hopes of little girls, stuff like that. He gets to the dreamcrusher, opens it, and as Hope watched, *all* those toys and stuffed animals and precious prizes poured onto the floor around her. She's just lost her 50 cents right? She never wins at these things. And now all those beautiful, wonderful, attractive items that were being kept from her behind that plexiglas are now piled at her little feet.

Hope stands there looks at me as if to say, "Dad! What can I do about this?" Her sweet little girl voice and cute blue eyes could have maybe scored her a toy: "Excuse me, sir, I just put my 50 cents in a few minutes ago. Any chance I could...?"

But there the prizes were, at her fingertips, and she had to resist the temptation. It was a golden, once-in-a-lifetime opportunity. And she resisted.

Now, obviously that's a pretty tame little example of the kinds of temptation you and I face. However, we both know that the crane game is wide open for us every day, isn't it? Plenty of temptations at our fingertips all the time. They're a click away; they're a look away; they're a question away; they're a thought away.

Temptations surround us. Will we resist? And how? We won't just accidentally keep ourselves from falling for temptation, as I'm sure you've figured out by now. Yet resisting it is a vital part of joining the Resistance. **We simply cannot afford to succumb to temptation. There's too much at stake, and our future's too bright.**

> **WE SIMPLY CANNOT AFFORD TO SUCCUMB TO TEMPTATION. THERE'S TOO MUCH AT STAKE, AND OUR FUTURE'S TOO BRIGHT.**

As we covered in the last chapter, it begins with our refusal to take these matters lightly or to be duped into thinking that forgiveness from God somehow means our choices and behaviors no longer matter. We realize each decision sets direction. And now we're specifically talking about the point of decision we call temptation. Let's look at what Scripture teaches us about this.

JESUS IS WITH US. HE ADDS HIS DIVINITY TO OUR HUMANITY.

Amazingly, the Bible says Jesus has felt what we feel. And He's dealt with what we deal with. "For we do not have a high priest who is unable to empathize with our weaknesses, but we have one who has been tempted in every way, just as we are—yet he did not sin." (Hebrews 4:15) Jesus is fully divine *and* fully human. So He's is not separated from us or our experience. He's *with* us in every sense of the term. In fact, that's the whole point, a great distinctive of this Way. Unlike various human-centered religions in which people try to attain union with the divine through meditation or good karma, here we see the glorious truth that the divine has chosen to unite completely with us—skin and all. As we remind ourselves each Christmas: "'The virgin will conceive and give birth to a son, and they will call him Immanuel' (which means 'God with us')." (Matthew 1:23)

And catch this (because sometimes we can get sideways on it): If Jesus was tempted, yet did not sin, that means being tempted is not a sin. Experiencing temptation does not make us any less like Jesus, who also dealt with every kind of temptation. It makes us human, just as He was.

Jesus batted a thousand, we never will. But hear this: season after season our batting average can rise and rise. It's what you and I do in that moment, in each moment of temptation—and the strength and habits we build *in those moments*—that makes all the difference. That's why this is a point worth hammering home. My prayer is that refreshing ourselves on these realities will save us from a world of hurt and heartache.

> **OUR FIRST MILES ON THIS HOLY PATH WILL BE BESET BY STUMBLES AND FALLS, BUT WHEN WE STICK WITH IT WE FIND SOON ENOUGH WE'RE RUNNING IN THE PATH OF HIS COMMANDS.**

C.S. Lewis is, of course, renown as a writer and thinker who has influenced countless people in recent decades. He also replied to every letter anyone wrote to him. Late in his life, Lewis wrote back to someone who had asked him about dealing with temptation:

> Of course I have had and still have plenty of temptations. Frequent and regular prayer, and frequent and regular Communions, are a great help, whether they *feel* at the time as if they were doing you good or whether they don't.
> ...Perhaps, however, the most important thing is to *keep on*: not to be discouraged however often one yields to the temptation, but always to pick yourself up again and ask forgiveness.

There it is: keep on. Keep to the Way. That's what counts most in this endeavor. Our first miles on this holy path will be beset by stumbles and falls, but when we stick with it we find soon enough we're running in the path of His commands (see Psalm 119:32). Lewis goes on by providing this piece of practical advice:

> We must learn by experience to avoid either trains of thought or social situations which *for us* (not necessarily for everyone) lead to temptations. Like motoring—don't wait till the last moment before you put on the brakes but put them on, gently and quietly, while the danger is still a good way off.[1]

When we walk with Jesus—Jesus with us in all our moments—on that good Way, we rightly see these temptations and recognize them for what they are. And in wisdom He guides us to tap the brakes and steer clear. This leads us to our second scriptural lesson.

Watch and pray. Spiritual laziness never yields personal holiness.

On the night of His arrest, in the hours before His capture, Jesus wanted to pray. He told his weary disciples, "Watch and pray so that you will not fall into temptation. The spirit is willing, but the flesh is weak." (Matthew 26:41 and Mark 14:38) We may tell ourselves that while this was a pivotal and unique moment in history, that's not us. We're not in the garden guarding Jesus from the mob and His accusers and a betraying kiss. And this is where we fool ourselves most grievously. Do we really think Jesus is only talking *to* the eleven and not *about* us? All of us as human beings?

Are there not forces at play in our world today who delight in seeing the Son of God silenced and His message mocked? Do we believe there are no false accusers? No betrayers? Are we not at our own pivotal moment in history? Do we not face such moments in our own personal histories? Jesus' words to those who had come for Him in the garden that fateful night can be

> **WHEN WE WALK WITH JESUS ON THAT GOOD WAY, WE RIGHTLY SEE TEMPTATIONS AND RECOGNIZE THEM FOR WHAT THEY ARE.**

rightly spoken to many corners of our world today: "This is your hour—when darkness reigns." (Luke 22:53)

"Stay awake. Stay alert," we hear Jesus saying. When we don't we *will* fall into temptation. We sleepwalk spiritually and sooner or later we slip and fall. Our willpower and best intentions are simply not enough. We must pay attention and pray alertly as Jesus taught:

> Don't let us yield to temptation, but rescue us from the evil one. (Matthew 6:13 NLT)
>
> Keep us clear of temptation, and save us from evil. (Ph)
>
> Keep us safe from ourselves and the Devil. (MSG)

This must be our daily prayer, prayed with eyes wide open. Always aware, one foot over the brake, alert to the world around us.

Let's ask an important question: How do we short-circuit temptation? If every one of us as human beings faces this as even Jesus did, then it deserves our consideration: How do we face such moments and prepare for them as they come to us daily?

Dan Ariely is a behavioral economist and Duke University psychology professor. He studies cheating—when and why we do it and when and why we don't.[2] After the Enron debacle of 2001, he started asking: How can well-intentioned people rationalize such unethical behavior? Most people just assumed this crisis of conscience was due to a few bad apples at the top. But it turned out that hundreds of people—accountants, managers, consultants—were all in on it, and most had convinced themselves it was fine or even for the greater good. Ariely observes:

> **OUR WILLPOWER AND BEST INTENTIONS ARE SIMPLY NOT ENOUGH. WE MUST PAY ATTENTION AND PRAY ALERTLY.**

> At one hand we all want to look ourselves in the mirror and feel good about ourselves, so we don't want to cheat. On the other hand, we could cheat a little bit and still feel good about ourselves. ...We call this a personal fudge factor.

How's that for a scientific term? "A personal fudge factor"...and we all have one. We perceive there's some reward in the cheating, but there's also the downside of guilt. So how much cheating can we do and still feel okay about ourselves? That was his team's researchable question.

So they did an experiment: Subjects have five minutes to take a math test. They get paid for every correct answer. Each turns in his or her completed test and is paid accordingly. Average correct? Four. This is the control group.

But another group was, as the experimenters put it, "tempted to cheat" and told: "After you take the test we will give you the correct answers so you can grade yourself. You are to then place your answer sheet in this shredder (which didn't actually shred) and report your number of correct answers so you can get paid." Suddenly subjects are smarter. Average number of correct answers according to the test-takers? Seven. The lesson: When people are incentivized to cheat, most will, at least some.

Then the researchers began to ask, "Now, how would you test a personal fudge factor? What can we do to shrink it?" Here's what they did next.

The researchers took two groups and tempted them both to cheat as the second group had been before. But before the math test they asked one group to try to recall the titles of up to ten books they read in high school. They asked the other group to recall as many of the Ten Commandments as they could. Ariely summarized their findings: "The moment people thought about trying to recall the Ten Commandments they stop cheating. ...So it's basically all about what you are thinking about." That's profound, and also no news to us. I can hear Paul's words, "Whatever is true...if anything is excellent or praiseworthy—think about such things." (Philippians 4:8) It's all about what you're thinking about.

> **IF OUR MINDS ARE FOCUSED ON TRUTH, OUR RATIONALIZATIONS AND EXCUSES FOR SIN WILL SOUND LIKE THE LIES AND FOOLISHNESS THEY REALLY ARE.**

It wasn't that the more religious people—the people who remembered the commandments—cheated less, and the irreligious people—the people who couldn't remember almost any commandments—cheated more. It turns out when people just *attempted* to recall the Ten Commandments—were just simply reminded that such an ethical code exists—and were then given the opportunity to cheat, they did not cheat at all. Not once. Ariely concludes:

> *At the moment* you can get people to think more deeply about honesty, to be more attentive, it does change your own understanding of what's right and wrong and your ability to rationalize in *that moment.* It's almost like an anti-rationalization mechanism. (*emphasis* mine)

Wow, that's perfect. I can't say it better myself. If our minds are focused on truth (even truth we can't always fully remember or articulate!), our rationalizations and excuses for sin will sound to us like the lies and foolishness they really are.

In the moment of temptation do we rationalize? Of course we do. (We know that voice can get loud and convincing.)

> **THE HOLY SPIRIT IN US AND OUR COOPERATION WITH HIM STRENGTHENS US AGAINST THE CONTAGION OF TEMPTATION.**

But we can move past that. In the moments and days and nights leading to our temptations we can live to remember the right and true Word of God. We're tapping the brakes, staying alert, remaining aware. This study only reinforces what the Bible says: We can resist and overcome temptation when we focus on what's right and true and ethical and beautiful. "I gain understanding from your precepts; therefore I hate every wrong path." (Psalm 119:104)

LOOK FOR THE WAY OUT. NOTHING IS INEVITABLE; WE ALWAYS HAVE A CHOICE.

Remember: we're developing *a resistance to* temptation. Is that even possible? In Jesus, it absolutely is. We can be stronger against temptation today than we were yesterday. Not every temptation, every time for the rest of your lives, but just as we can develop a resistance to viruses or sickness—though it doesn't mean we'll never catch cold—the Holy Spirit in us and our cooperation with Him by keeping to the Way absolutely strengthens us against the contagion of temptation. Paul put it to the Corinthians like this:

> No temptation has overtaken you except what is common to mankind. And God is faithful; he will not let you be tempted beyond what you can bear. But when you are tempted, he will also provide a way out so that you can endure it. (1 Corinthians 10:13)

What is that way out? The power, finally, to choose. You see, when it comes to fleeing temptation and obeying Christ, we each face the choice between *can't* and *won't*. We may think we can't resist temptation, as if we have no choice. But the fact is, when I give in to temptation it's because I've decided I *won't* resist any longer, if at all.

Those who aren't yet Christians have every right and reason to use *can't*, because they really can't! Without Christ and His power, they lack what it takes to change permanently, just as we did without Him. But people with the power of Christ? There's no *can't* left for us. Pastor and author Chuck Swindoll frames it like this to his fellow Christians:

> Hey, let's face it; we don't because we won't...we disobey because we want to, not because we have to...because we choose to, not because we're forced to. The sooner we are willing to own up realistically to our responsibility and stop playing the blame game at pity parties for ourselves, the more we'll learn and change and the less we'll burn and blame. ...We're really saying "I won't," because we don't choose to say "With the help of God, I will!"[3]

> **THERE MAY BE REASONS, BUT IF YOU'RE A JESUS-FOLLOWER THERE ARE NO MORE EXCUSES FOR ANY INDIVIDUAL SIN.**

We can indeed tell ourselves, "My story does not have to include that sin, me falling for that temptation." I've known far too many people who've resigned themselves to the idea that they only learn lessons the hard way—a telling phrase—and that "resistance is futile." Don't believe it.

Please understand: I'm not trying to paint an overly rosy picture here. There may be many reasons that lead to our falling for temptation, many very real factors involved in our bad decisions. But if you're a Jesus-follower, there are no excuses for any individual sin. Reasons, yes—and part of our growth and transformation in Christ is dealing with those reasons (trauma, abuse, lots of things that can weaken us, things from which we need healed and delivered.) There are lots of potential reasons, but no more excuses. We have new power in our corner. We have "a way out," the narrow Way, the Way of Jesus.

Even though we're never sinless, we can choose to sin less and less. And no single sin is inevitable. We must realize and remember this. As we deal with the moment of temptation, we have choices. They are ours and only ours to make.

Know the stakes. Our fidelity matters and affects many futures.

Sometimes we can think, "I'm just one person. No one's really affected by what I do, by these personal ethical decisions I make. Yes, I may put myself at risk, but that's my call and my business." We kid ourselves. The fact is, there's a lot at stake in our decisions. There's no easy way to say it. We have to face it. Our selfish decisions can injure ourselves and others deeply. Our foolish actions dishonor our Lord and can discredit His Gospel. We keep the Way and join the Resistance not only for ourselves but to

> **WE JOIN THE RESISTANCE NOT ONLY FOR OURSELVES BUT TO FORGE A PATH AND CREATE A SPACE FOR OTHERS TO SEE THE GOODNESS OF GOD.**

forge and path and create a space for others to see the goodness of God. Paul provides the proper focus: "Whatever you do, do it all for the glory of God. Do not cause anyone to stumble." (1 Corinthians 10:31-32)

Peter warns his readers of this self-inflicted delusion: "Many will follow their depraved conduct and will bring the way of truth into disrepute." (2 Peter 2:2) He's talking about Christians who leave the Way. They fall, but don't follow Lewis' advice: they don't get up, ask for forgiveness, and return to the Way. Instead, they follow another way, their own way. One bad choice leads to another and these believers follow to see where this path will take them. Whenever this is allowed to happen, the true Way is discredited.

A little later Peter is even more emphatic: "It would have been better for them not to have known the way of righteousness, than to have known it and then to turn their backs on the sacred command that was passed on to them." (2 Peter 2:21) To know the Way is a precious gift; to follow Jesus is a great privilege. When we begin to de-value this great gift, when we begin to turn our back on this wise path, we are committing the most tragic of sins: letting go of the most valuable thing we've ever been given and ever had.

How does this happen? And how can we see to it that this tragedy doesn't happen in us? I've found that such a turning away is virtually always the result of a diluted vision of the Way of Jesus, a vision that sees it less as a way of life worthy on its own merits of our wholehearted commitment and more as a way of covering our spiritual or religious bases. John R.W. Stott gives this convicting analysis in his book, *Basic Christianity*:

> In countries to which Christian civilization has spread, large numbers of people have covered themselves with a decent, but thin, veneer of Christianity. They have allowed themselves to become somewhat involved, enough to be respectable but not enough to be uncomfortable. Their religion is a great, soft cushion. It protects them from the hard unpleasantness of life, while changing its place and shape to suit their convenience. No wonder the cynics speak of hypocrites in the church and dismiss religion as escapism. The message of Jesus was very different. He never lowered his standards or modified his conditions to make his call more readily acceptable. He asked his first disciples, and he has asked every disciple since, to give him their thoughtful and total commitment. Nothing less than this will do.[4]

> **JESUS IS REAL AND PRESENT. THIS IS PERSONAL, AND THE MOMENT IT CEASES TO BE SO IS A SERIOUS MOMENT INDEED.**

What Stott describes here is epidemic among us American Christians. We see our faith as an app that keeps us in God's good graces or a protection plan that keeps us insured against harm while we live as we choose.

More than all this, what does our conscious choosing of sin (make no mistake, that's ultimately what we're talking about) say to our Lord Jesus? He is very real and very present. This is personal, and the moment it ceases to be is for us a serious moment indeed. Forgiveness is always available, but it can't be taken lightly. It comes to us at a high cost—paid by Jesus on the cross. And forgiveness doesn't protect us or those around us from the consequences of our choices. It's an empty rationalization that fools us into thinking there's not a lot at stake. Our fidelity matters—more than words can fully express.

This chapter provides some sober reminders to us keepers of the Way. Joining the Resistance doesn't at all mean we'll never fall, but it does mean getting back up and keeping to the Way. We won't follow our sin wherever it leads (nowhere good) or even (it's possible) turn our backs on the good and right Way of Jesus He's paved for us by His death on the cross.

> **FORGIVENESS DOESN'T PROTECT US OR THOSE AROUND US FROM THE CONSEQUENCES OF OUR CHOICES. SO MUCH IS AT STAKE.**

Friend, every day you face moments of decision that can become pivotal points in your life story. My prayer is that you would approach these junctures of temptation with wisdom and foresight and be rescued from the heartache of poor choices. We can spare ourselves and those near us a world of hurt by being prepared for such moments, tuning ourselves to the truth each day.

Jesus is with us, so we can watch and pray and look for the way out of the darkness that creeps in around us. We simply cannot afford to succumb to temptation. There's too much at stake and our future's too bright.

> WATCH AND PRAY SO THAT
> YOU WILL NOT FALL INTO TEMPTATION.
> THE SPIRIT IS WILLING, BUT THE FLESH IS WEAK.
> [MATTHEW 26:41 AND MARK 14:38]

Our Resistance is an active, never a passive, endeavor. Remember: we're developing *a resistance to* temptation. We're walking out our salvation with a prayerful determination to stand and not fall. This doesn't happen by accident. It requires consistently conditioning ourselves and intentionally strengthening our weaknesses.

This is worthy of our consideration: What am I actively, purposefully doing to get spiritually stronger? How am I disciplining myself so I no longer fall for sin's tricks and into its traps?

> **CONQUERING TEMPTATION REQUIRES VIGILANCE. SPIRITUAL LAZINESS NEVER YIELDS PERSONAL HOLINESS.**

---WE PRAY---

"Jesus, I pray all day with my eyes wide open and focused on You."

GOD IS FAITHFUL; HE WILL NOT LET YOU BE TEMPTED BEYOND WHAT YOU CAN BEAR. BUT WHEN YOU ARE TEMPTED, HE WILL ALSO PROVIDE A WAY OUT SO THAT YOU CAN ENDURE IT.
[1 CORINTHIANS 10:13]

As Christians, we are no longer slaves to sin, no longer destined to succumb to temptation. In Christ we are provided a power to endure in righteousness. This is essential to our Resistance, truly what it's all about.

If we—even after we become followers of Jesus—believe we are powerless to make right choices amidst temptation, then we are stunting our growth in this new life. Envision yourself always with a righteous and healthy option, no matter the temptation. Start now: What can I do today to begin exercising that option at each critical decision point in my walk?

> **WHILE IT'S TRUE THAT WE'RE NEVER SINLESS, NO SINGLE SIN IS EVER INEVITABLE. WE ALWAYS HAVE A CHOICE.**

---WE PRAY---

"God, thank You for guarding and guiding me from wrong choices."

> FOR WE DO NOT HAVE A HIGH PRIEST WHO IS UNABLE TO EMPATHIZE WITH OUR WEAKNESSES, BUT WE HAVE ONE WHO HAS BEEN TEMPTED IN EVERY WAY, JUST AS WE ARE—YET HE DID NOT SIN.
> [HEBREWS 4:15]

Our weaknesses are no surprise to God. He understands. The God-man, Jesus Christ, also encountered and endured our very human temptations and pressures. Completely full of the Spirit, He shows us what those with the Spirit are capable of: namely, victory over sin and temptation. Though in this life we'll never fully reach His capabilities, we can—and should—grow closer and closer to them.

Ask yourself: How would Jesus respond to the temptations I face? Can I follow His example?

> **JESUS IS FULLY HUMAN AND FULLY DIVINE. HE WALKS WITH US IN OUR HUMANITY AND BESTOWS ON US HIS DIVINITY.**

———WE PRAY———

"Lord Jesus, I follow You by following Your example."

Many will follow their depraved conduct and will bring the way of truth into disrepute.
[2 Peter 2:2]

Our choices are not without consequences. And no sin is ever harmless or fully a "private matter." When we reduce our resistance and step off the Way, we are not only taking a trail to our own downfall, but leading others astray.

It can be easy to slide into the deception that our ethical behavior doesn't really matter, that only our sincere belief counts. But this artificial separation of character and creed does untold damage not only to our souls, but to the credibility of the Gospel and thus others' spiritual progress.

Consider: What does my way of life communicate to others about the new life I've found in Jesus?

> **WHEN WE SLIDE BACK INTO OUR SIN, WE HURT NOT ONLY OURSELVES AND OTHERS, BUT THE REPUTATION OF CHRIST.**

---WE PRAY---

"Father, let me not cause others to misunderstand You by my poor choices."

> IT WOULD HAVE BEEN BETTER FOR THEM NOT TO HAVE KNOWN THE WAY OF RIGHTEOUSNESS, THAN TO HAVE KNOWN IT AND THEN TO TURN THEIR BACKS ON THE SACRED COMMAND THAT WAS PASSED ON TO THEM.
> [2 PETER 2:21]

Walking this sacred "way of righteousness" is not to be taken lightly. While our salvation is never a precarious thing at risk of being lost due to our latest misstep, it is also not something to be taken for granted as if our unfaithfulness is inconsequential. Throughout Scripture our relationship with God is likened to marriage, repeatedly emphasizing the beauty of our fidelity and the tragedy of our infidelity.

God is always faithful. Reflect on your faithfulness to Him and ask: What kind of "spouse" have I been to God?

SAYING YES TO FOLLOWING JESUS MEANS COMMITTING TO WALKING FORWARD WITH HIM FAITHFULLY EVERY DAY.

—WE PRAY—

"Lord, help me not lose sight of what's at stake when following You."

Lead us not into temptation, but deliver us from the evil one.
[Matthew 6:13]

We're never alone in our Resistance. We have a power in our corner that is ever only a prayer away. In His model prayer Jesus included this pivotal request: Guide us away from temptation by drawing us to You. This prayer of reliance and realignment is a constant practice in the life of a disciple.

The evil one, whom we'll consider more in our next chapter, is not found on the Way of Christ, but instead runs alongside it working hard to distract and dissuade those who follow it. Since this is true, ask yourself: Am I watching my step and relying on God to rescue me from the evil that nips at my heels?

> **WE FIND DELIVERANCE FROM THE POWERFUL PULL OF DARKNESS THROUGH OUR PRAYERFUL RELIANCE ON GOD.**

---WE PRAY---

"Father, I rely on You and Your power every day."

4
STAY IN THE FIGHT

I'm inspired by the story of a college freshman from the church I serve. Her name is Ally.

On campus at Indiana University she and many of the student body encountered a pair of men stationed near a confluence of busy sidewalks loudly preaching hate and condemning every person who walked by. They referred to themselves as "God's Judges" and spitefully singled out passersby from the growing crowd. Through the placards they held they called women names I won't reprint here.

Some students listened and many tried to ignore them, but Ally countered them. She took chalk and wrote on the sidewalk in front of them the words in her heart: "Jesus loves everyone." The angry sidewalk preacher vehemently shamed her, calling her terrible names. "He used every derogatory word he could think of," she told me. "Proclaiming it in the name of Jesus, saying he was trying to help me see the wrongs of my ways. His reasons were so far from the Truth." But the sidewalk chalk wasn't the extent of Ally's resistance...

> I prayed and praised God. I prayed for him and prayed for those listening not to let the hatred and misguidance into their hearts. Christianity is not about hate. Jesus does not hate you or anyone else. And before I knew it I realized I was speaking out loud to everyone. To him. To myself.

It was God working through me. It was God giving me scripture and love and the courage to share the Word. God's powers are innumerable and His love is everlasting. He loves all of His children. He loves me and He loves you, too. God is love.

In this chapter we're going to learn again what Ally seems to know so well: **We keep to the Way and join the Resistance by remaining aware of and armed against the spiritual forces of darkness and evil.** We don't forget there is a fight to be fought.

That's right, I said "spiritual forces of darkness and evil." There is a spiritual realm that's at least as real as the physical. We miss much when we underestimate or ignore this reality. Spiritual forces are at work in the world, powerful forces of light and influential forces of darkness. And it's been that way since the beginning.

These evil forces always seek to deceive humankind and veer us away from God and His truth and Way. Recall these suspicious words of the devil in the earliest scenes of the human story: "Did God really say...?" (Genesis 3:1), he asked Adam and Eve, calling into question and then twisting ever so slightly God's good guidance.

God their Father had given direction to Adam and Eve; He set boundaries. Their decision to take a different direction began with believing the devil's deception and twisted truth about those boundaries. Is God good? Does He know what He's doing? Can He be trusted? Is He worthy of our allegiance? Such questions are the well-worn tools of the evil one. It's his area of expertise: to take a truth and drain it of some of its most essential meaning, give it a little twist and see if we'll accept it. But please remember and never forget: half truths are whole lies. Our first mistake is giving ear to them.

> **HALF TRUTHS ARE WHOLE LIES. OUR FIRST MISTAKE IS GIVING EAR TO THEM.**

This is not a challenge of only ages past; it is a constant engagement for us as keepers of the Way today. As the Corinthian Christians experienced this test, Paul expressed his concern with words we each need to hear. He saw what was happening and cited the opening scenes of Eden's garden as ones which play themselves out again and again:

> But I am afraid that just as Eve was deceived by the serpent's cunning, your minds may somehow be led astray from your sincere and pure devotion to Christ. For if someone comes to you and preaches a Jesus other than the Jesus we preached, or if you receive a different spirit from the Spirit you received, or a different gospel from the one you accepted, you put up with it easily enough. (2 Corinthians 11:3-4)

The "serpent's cunning" always aims to deceive our minds. Satan's schemes invariably include influencing our thoughts, which ideas we accept and reject, and the way we see the world. If we can be "led astray" and off the Way—even by just a degree or two—we'll soon find ourselves in a distant and wild territory far from truth.

Paul was concerned about these Christians. They had a lot of humanness going on in their church and in their lives. And in their fallen humanness, they were susceptible to false teachers. Paul was afraid they may be deceived just as our original parents were, by some twisted truth and wrong ways of looking at God and the world. He understood this would dilute and even derail their sincere love of and obedience to Jesus. Paul knew what he was up against. In both Eden and Corinth, he saw the source of this falsehood as satanic.

> **SATAN'S SCHEMES INVARIABLY INCLUDE INFLUENCING OUR THOUGHTS, WHICH IDEAS WE ACCEPT AND REJECT, AND THE WAY WE SEE THE WORLD.**

Paul was constantly countering such "false teachers" who preached a different gospel from a different spirit about a different Jesus. Maybe they were preachers of hate such as Ally confronted. Or perhaps they were the all-too-common legalists who preached that grace must be earned. Whatever they preached, we can be sure they kept parts of some truths and let go of others and in the mix made sure they majored on some minors. Paul was sensitive to such false ideas. We should be too. Their recipe hasn't changed.

But the deeper problem in Paul's estimation was not the false teaching itself, but that these believers "put up with it easily enough." They may not have accepted it wholly, but they didn't reject it either. They didn't call it for what it really was and get it out of their heads and hearts. Paul knew this could cause them to fall just as Eve (and Adam) did. "Don't you know that a little yeast leavens the whole batch of dough?" (1 Corinthians 5:6) he asked these same Christians in his earlier letter. The little we let in, the mere foothold we give, can quickly affect everything.

"You're putting up with stuff you shouldn't," Paul is essentially saying. "And it's going to be your downfall if you're not careful." As it says in Romans 14:22, we can condemn ourselves by what we approve, by the wrong ideas we put up with, by what we *tolerate*. It is in this push and pull of ideas, of philosophies and worldviews, I believe the most significant spiritual battles of our day are fought—both in our own minds and in our world at large.

> **IT IS IN THIS PUSH AND PULL OF IDEAS THAT THE MOST SIGNIFICANT SPIRITUAL BATTLES OF OUR DAY ARE WON AND LOST.**

Keepers of the Way have been engaged in discerning truth from error since the beginning. Irenaeus, an early Church Father, reminds us: "Error, indeed, is never set forth in its *naked deformity*, lest, being thus exposed, it should at once be detected."[1] That's why the lies of the devil are most often a clever concoction of palatable half-truths, sweet to the taste, but deadly to digest. However, the battle is ours to win if we will but acknowledge it and enter the fray.

Truth is at hand. Nothing can replace God's Word.

In this fracas of ideas, it is gratifying to know that truth is accessible. This is not a puzzle we must solve, a difficult pop quiz we may never quite pass. Truth is an actuality, and absolutely available to us in God's Word. This is not a tenuous thing. We can trust the Scriptures and move forward in confidence and with fortitude. "Heaven and earth will pass away," Jesus assured, "but my words will never pass away." (Luke 21:33)

Jesus told a parable about the truth of the Gospel falling on human hearts just as seed falls on different types of soil. He described one particular condition of heart/soil pertinent to our discussion:

> Some fell along the path; it was trampled on, and the birds ate it up. ...Those along the path are the ones who hear, and then the devil comes and takes away the word from their hearts, so that they may not believe and be saved. (Luke 8:5,12)

This captures the essence of the battles we face as keepers of the Way.

We are walking through life, encountering Jesus, following Jesus, receiving His Word, but like a bird pecking at seed along a path, the devil—like the thief he is—aims always to snatch that Word, God's truth, from us. We seek to listen and learn. Satan seeks to steal. This is the case not only when we *first hear*, but also as we *keep hearing*.

However, we're not passive victims here. We can strengthen our grip on God's Word and pay attention to the competing ways of thinking that can try to stake a claim on our mental real estate. "We demolish arguments and every pretension that sets itself up against the knowledge of God, and we take captive every thought to make it obedient to Christ." (2 Corinthians 10:5) Our spiritual battles are fought along the neural pathways of our minds.

> **WE CAGE EVERY WILD BIRD, EVERY ERRANT THOUGHT, THAT TRIES TO PERCH IN THE BRANCHES OF OUR MINDS.**

"The knowledge of God," as Paul puts it, is the true Gospel, the Good News of Jesus and His loving grace. It's what paves the Way. And we keep to it, but there are perspectives, ways of thinking that want to set themselves up to compete against that Way. Paul essentially says, "We see these pretentious arguments for the flimsy roadblocks they are and we steamroll through them. We take captive anything other than Christ that would seek to captivate us. We cage every wild bird, every errant thought, that tries to perch in the branches of our minds." No tolerance for half truth, no room for falsehood. That's our pledge, that's our goal.

Modern godless philosophies contort truth, mixing in things that sound good while removing the parts that get in the way of our preferences. Here are just a few examples:

> It's popular to declare that God is love, but we rarely remind each other that God is holy. However, both are equally true and each fact has its profound implications.

> People often quote "Judge not" (Matthew 7:1) but easily ignore "Produce fruit in keeping with repentance." (Luke 3:8) Our world forgets that immediately after Jesus said to the accusing crowd that only those without sin should cast stones, He turned to the accused and instructed, "Go and leave your life of sin." (John 8:11)

> We love to hear that God wants to prosper us and give us our best life now. Such partial-truths satisfy itching ears and promote wishful thinking. But no sloganeer prints "in this world you will have trouble" (John 16:33) on a bumper sticker or greeting card.

> We excuse sin (if the word is even used) with quips like "Nobody's perfect" and "I'm only human" and "Grace abounds" without also confronting the brutal fact that "those who live like this will not inherit the kingdom of God." (Galatians 5:21) We misread and cheapen the Gospel because we want to believe God will conveniently neutralize the consequences of our choices.

I realize all-too-well what I've shared above can sound abrasive—or perhaps smug and self-righteous—to ears conditioned by the belief we can choose our own truth. But in the marketplace of ideas, keepers of the Way see that certain truths cannot be edited because they're inconvenient or deleted because they're uncomfortable. Certainly not if we are to acknowledge God and seek to follow Him. He is God; we rejoice in that fact. And as God, He gets to define truth, including what's right and wrong, healthy and unhealthy, good and bad.

Attorney and author Kristi Burton Brown recently wrote an article entitled, "Modern Christians and the Dumbing Down of Sin." I resonate with the feelings she describes:

> It can be disappointing to hang out with modern Christians today. For all the emphasis on love, grace, and happiness, we seem to have forgotten that sin is real. Sin doesn't change because our culture changes. Sin doesn't change because our friends do it or because we struggle with it. Sin is always sin, and it's really that simple.[2]

Such a view is hardly popular. As our culture accepts and even celebrates what used to be considered sin, I've regularly seen people—even self-described Christians—post on social media statements such as, "It's the twenty-first century, people! Get with the times." as if the calendar could change the insight, the command, the wisdom of an eternal, holy God or that somehow we now know better.

Let's all check our bibles for an expiration date. Can't find one? Nope, me neither.

This psalmist's prayer becomes our own: "I seek you with all my heart; do not let me stray from your commands. I have hidden your word in my heart that I might not sin against you." (Psalm 119:10-11) Don't let me stray. Keep me to the Way. I'll hide in my heart Your Word like a seed deeply planted, far from any thieving fowl, where no bird, no devil can pluck it up. Why? Because I don't want to sin against You. This is our heart's cry.

SATAN HAS LIMITS. HE ONLY GOES WHERE WE GIVE HIM ROOM.

Paul put it to the Ephesians very simply: "Do not give the devil a foothold." (Ephesians 4:27) Don't give him room, any entrance into your life, mind, or heart. No space where he can put even his toe in the door. It's solid advice not frequently followed. Satan finds his way in. Who gives this devil such a point of entry? We do. How? By letting half-truth become our truth, by disengaging from the work of discerning what's true and what's not.

Joining the Resistance means thinking twice and thinking through the philosophies, beliefs, and worldviews we absorb and accept. It also means that when truth's reality confronts us, we aren't closed to it by our own selfishness and soft-mindedness.

Consider Peter's words: "Be alert and of sober mind. Your enemy the devil prowls around like a roaring lion looking for someone to devour." (1 Peter 5:8) There's a link between our state of mind and our ability to deal with the devil, who's always looking for some dim soul with their guard down so he can eat them alive and destroy their life.

Be alert and of sober—thoughtful, discerning—mind. Engage with your thinking, pay attention to what's happening in your head. The devil wants to keep us light and fluffy and distracted—lacking conviction regarding our beliefs. In fact, I'm observing today that what many mean by "my beliefs" are actually just a collection of memes and feel-good statements they want to believe are true. "These are my beliefs" or "Let me tell you what I believe," they might say. "Just believe" is the new faith, no matter what one believes in. Want your team to have a great season? "Just believe." Want life to turn out well? "You gotta have faith." What such beliefs contain or in whom such faith is placed is anyone's guess. But by no means should someone get specific or confuse us with some facts.

> **TRUE BELIEF IS A CONVICTION ABOUT WHAT IS REAL AND ACTUAL. SUCH BELIEF CAN COME THROUGH EARNEST LEARNING AS WELL AS HONEST FAITH.**

Comedian Louis C.K. declares in one of his routines: "I have a lot of beliefs and I live by none of them. That's just the way I am. They're just my beliefs. I just like believing them. They make me feel good about who I am. I like that part."[3] I think he speaks for a lot of people today for whom "beliefs" have become merely a set of inspirational statements, things we hope are true, wish were true, a personalized playlist entitled "this is what I believe."

True belief is a conviction about what is real and actual. Such beliefs can come from earnest learning as well as honest faith. They are not the same as hopes or wishes or dreams. Beliefs are our conclusions about reality. When we say we believe in Jesus we are saying we believe Jesus, that we have reached the conclusion that He is real and what He says is true and accurate. We believe Him. Such solid belief is a bulwark against Satan's arsenal of lies.

Dr. Martin Luther King Jr. knew something about trying to get Christians to solidify their convictions. Probably no Christian in modern history worked harder or sacrificed more to this end than he. Writing about the malady of what he called "soft thinking" in his book, *Strength to Love,* King observed:

> Rarely do we find men who willingly engage in hard, solid thinking. There is an almost universal quest for easy answers and half-baked solutions. Nothing pains some people more than having to think. …Few people have the toughness of mind to judge critically and to discern the true from the false, the fact from the fiction. Our minds are constantly being invaded by legions of half-truths, prejudices, and false facts. One of the great needs of mankind is to be lifted above the morass of false propaganda.[4]

> **WHEN WE SAY WE BELIEVE IN JESUS WE ARE SAYING WE BELIEVE JESUS, THAT WE'VE CONCLUDED WHAT HE SAYS IS TRUE AND ACCURATE.**

This is a powerful and painfully accurate description of the challenge before us. Keepers of the Way must cultivate the "toughness of mind" (or soberness of mind, as Peter put it) to rise to this challenge and resist the allure of "easy answers and half-baked solutions" that most make their own as they simply scroll, swipe, and skim through life.

It's been true since the beginning and it's no less true today. Satan never stops cranking out "false propaganda." But we must see through it. It's not easy. It takes some effort. We must be engaged. The current of our culture runs counter to "hard, solid thinking." Such thinking is essential to our calling. Soft-mindedness renders resistance impossible.

Recently *The Atlantic* ran an article called "The Coddling of the American Mind" that very thoughtfully explained a movement, driven largely by students, to scrub college campuses clean of words, ideas, and subjects that might cause discomfort or give offense, to be protected from any idea they don't like. It's creating a culture in which everyone must precisely weigh each word before speaking, lest they face charges of insensitivity, aggression, or worse.

"The thin argument 'I'm offended' becomes an unbeatable trump card," the writers observe. Once it's played, silence ensues and dialog ceases.

> What are we doing to our students if we encourage them to develop extra-thin skin in the years just before they leave the cocoon of adult protection and enter the workforce? ...Rather than trying to protect students from words and ideas that they will inevitably encounter, colleges should do all they can to equip students to thrive in a world full of words and ideas that they cannot control.[5]

Now let's be honest, it's not just today's college students for whom this is true. And I'm not so sure it's only colleges who bear the responsibility to do what the authors espouse; maybe churches should do the same: thicken our skin and ready our minds to rightly encounter and counter the confusing and conflictive ideas of our world. Our culture's new dogma is "Let me define my truth. I'll choose my own beliefs, like pets I find comforting. I'll collect mine you collect yours." In the meantime our minds are getting lazy, we're being coddled, and the devil laughs.

> **SATAN'S BUILT A BUBBLEGUM BUFFER AROUND ANY SHARP EDGES OF THE TRUTH. AND WE'RE GETTING SOFT.**

The truth is not always easy to hear. Christianity begins with some uncomfortable truths: The idea that I need to be forgiven means I have fallen short, that my inflated self-esteem might need a bit of a reality check. The concept of repentance means there's an ethic outside my opinion and what's "right for me" may not be right at all. Many find such ideas unpalatable or believe they make our faith harsh and humorless. But, in all candor, this is a perspective borne of immaturity and self-centeredness—two things this world desperately needs to shed. Satan has built a bubble gum buffer around any sharp edges of the truth. And we are, as a society, getting soft.

Ours is a position of power. We are victors, not victims.

When it comes to spiritual and dark forces, we are not powerless. Far from it. "Submit yourselves, then, to God," James exhorts. "Resist the devil, and he will flee from you." (James 4:7) Catch what he's saying here: Our humble, loving, steady submission to God—our keeping to the Way and joining the Resistance—is a thoroughly effective repellant of dark forces and their deception. We do the resisting; it's the devil who does the fleeing. We simply stand the ground the Lord has given each of us.

This was Paul's message as he closed his letter to the Ephesian Christians. There isn't a day we can afford to forget these words: "Be strong in the Lord and in his mighty power. Put on the full armor of God, so that you can take your stand against the devil's schemes." (Ephesians 6:10-11) *Stand*, a military metaphor for those victorious in battle, is used four times by Paul in this passage. "Take your stand," he charges. "Stand your ground," and "after you've done everything... stand." "Stand firm."

> **OUR HUMBLE, LOVING, STEADY SUBMISSION TO GOD IS A THOROUGHLY EFFECTIVE REPELLANT OF DARK FORCES AND THEIR DECEPTION.**

Against what are we standing? "The devil's schemes," his plans and machinations for our downfall. Those schemes always start with twisting our ideas of truth. Adam, Eve, you, me, and everyone in between.

Remember: Our enemy is real and forceful, but he and his minions are not omniscient, omnipotent, or omnipresent. We serve the only One who is. And we stand victoriously because—as Paul repeatedly emphasizes in Ephesians—God supplies "his incomparably great power for us who believe." (Ephesians 1:19) It is God "who is able to do immeasurably more than all we ask or imagine, according to his power that is at work within us." (Ephesians 3:20) We must "be strong in the Lord and in his mighty power." (Ephesians 6:10) Our risk of peril is not in fighting and losing—we've too much power for that—but in losing because we're not in the fight. I pray for you as Paul did for his readers, "that out of his glorious riches he may strengthen you with power through his Spirit in your inner being." (Ephesians 3:16)

What keeps us from this fight? Fear borne of misplaced trust. And distraction due to misplaced priorities. We're afraid because we look to sources other than God for our strength and confidence. We're weakened because we spend our energy on things that don't matter. Our guard is down and our resistance is low.

We feel victorious so long as our health and circumstances are preferable, the economy is good, and our government guarantees our freedoms. For American Christians, much is made of the growing trend of curtailing the free expression of religion. While this is concerning, it is far from consuming. Wherever it's headed, we can be certain it is not to our defeat. Our freedom is founded more deeply. "Though I am free and belong to no one, I have made myself a slave to everyone, to win as many as possible." (1 Corinthians 9:19) The future of the Church is not based on who sits in the White House, and our success is in no way dependent upon the cooperation of our society or government.

> **OUR RISK OF PERIL IS NOT IN FIGHTING AND LOSING—WE'VE TOO MUCH POWER FOR THAT—BUT IN LOSING BECAUSE WE'RE NOT IN THE FIGHT.**

Further, I've sat with countless believers who ask "Why me?" or "Why did God do this to me?" when misfortune or tragedy come their way. They have somehow embraced the idea that life is supposed to be smooth. They forget they're in a fight.

And when we forget we're in a fight, when we lose sight of the spiritual, eternal realities around us, we begin investing ourselves in the material and temporal. We find our joy in the stuff we purchase and our identity in the teams we cheer on and our significance in our physical attractiveness. We get confused about what truly matters. We pray primarily about things going well and not so much that God's will be done no matter what. We gather for worship more to feel better and recharge our batteries than to be better and get equipped to change the world. We mistake our earthly life for our whole life and we drown in the frivolous and banal.

There is much that's beautiful and enjoyable in this world, no doubt. And not everything is a battle. But for followers of Jesus, the Resistance is real and a certain level of disciplined wartime mentality is simply essential. As C.S. Lewis memorably put it in *Mere Christianity*:

> Enemy-occupied territory—that is what this world is. Christianity is the story of how the rightful king has landed, you might say, landed in disguise, and is calling us all to take place in a great campaign of sabotage.[6]

Though we'll talk more about this sabotage in our next section, suffice it to say that we Christians walk and work in a world unseen by most, one in which light is clashing with darkness, good is vigorously overcoming evil, and yes, the demonic is defeated by the angelic though the prayers we pray, the love we share, and the Way we keep. "For though we live in the world, we do not wage war as the world does. The weapons we fight with are not the weapons of the world." (2 Corinthians 10:3-4)

Keepers of the Way walk in power, the path we follow on this planet was forged by the very Son of God. Hell cowers at our steps and trembles at our approach. "Fear not" the people of God are repeatedly told. "The God of peace will soon crush Satan under your feet. " (Romans 16:20)

Whether we're countering 1) a lackadaisical version of Christianity that's dumbing down sin or 2) a thin-skinned culture that's coddling our minds or 3) a limp definition of accomplishment that keeps us running but going nowhere, remember: We have joined the Resistance. We won't back down.

Whether we're encountering sidewalk preachers of hate or the weak arguments that want to drain belief of conviction and fluff it up with convenience, we have joined the Resistance and won't back down. Because "if God is for us, who can be against us? ...We are more than conquerors through him who loved us." (Romans 8:31,37)

> SUBMIT YOURSELVES, THEN, TO GOD.
> RESIST THE DEVIL, AND HE WILL FLEE FROM YOU.
> [JAMES 4:7]

Some people ascribe to the devil far too much power and live in fear of him. Others underestimate him to the point of ignoring his existence. Neither approach is healthy or accurate. Satan is certainly real and his aim is definitely our destruction, but when we stand our ground in the Resistance, he's the one who runs away.

A heart fully submitted to the Lord is the most effective demonic repellent. We are wise to examine ourselves and ask: Are there areas of my life I've yet to fully submit to the Lordship of Christ? Are there outposts of independence I'm harboring for myself? Am I ready for complete, unconditional surrender?

> **OUR ONGOING SUBMISSION TO GOD BRINGS PROTECTION FROM AND POWER OVER THE FORCES OF DARKNESS.**

—WE PRAY—

"God, I submit myself to You. I have no other master."

DO NOT GIVE THE DEVIL A FOOTHOLD.
[EPHESIANS 4:27]

Unsurrendered areas of our lives are open invitations to Satan's influence, whether we consciously realize this or not. Much is at stake. We must give him no shelter, for he's never satisfied until he has torn down our whole house.

This is up to us. In the end, the only power the devil has over us is power we give him. Keeping up our Resistance means setting a guard at the gateways of our hearts and minds. We must be self-aware: What and whom do I allow to influence me? From what and whom do I choose to learn what's right and wrong, wise and unwise, healthy and unhealthy? To whom have I granted the power to engage my emotions and inform my thinking?

> **THE FORCES OF DARKNESS ARE ALWAYS LOOKING FOR EVEN THE SLIGHTEST ENTRANCE INTO OUR HEARTS.**

---WE PRAY---

"Holy Spirit, fill every part of my heart so there's room for nothing else."

> THOSE ALONG THE PATH ARE THE ONES WHO HEAR,
> AND THEN THE DEVIL COMES AND TAKES AWAY
> THE WORD FROM THEIR HEARTS, SO THAT
> THEY MAY NOT BELIEVE AND BE SAVED.
> [LUKE 8:12]

We lose our way most quickly when we lose our grip on God's Word. Its truth saves and sets free as we believe it. That's why Satan loves to steal it from us and replace it with lies. Indeed, he is a thief and a liar.

It's so essential to our Resistance that we get into the Bible and get the Bible into us. Like good nutrition, it fortifies us against the forces out to distract and defeat us. We must keep ourselves full of its wise truth. Consider your spiritual diet: Am I feasting regularly on Scripture?

> **WE KEEP GOD'S WORD IN OUR HEARTS AND WE KEEP OUR GUARD UP AGAINST THE DEVIL AND HIS THIEVERY.**

---WE PRAY---

"Christ, I cling to Your good Word and will not let it go."

> WE DEMOLISH ARGUMENTS AND EVERY PRETENSION
> THAT SETS ITSELF UP AGAINST THE KNOWLEDGE OF
> GOD, AND WE TAKE CAPTIVE EVERY THOUGHT
> TO MAKE IT OBEDIENT TO CHRIST.
> [2 CORINTHIANS 10:5]

In fighting the good fight of faith, our victory or defeat is often determined by what we think—the actual thoughts we allow in our minds. Keeping up our Resistance means keeping our focus on Christ, His truth and His ways. Our thoughts can betray us; not everything we think is correct or helpful. We must discern what thoughts are worth keeping and which should be dismissed.

Have you ever thought about your thinking? Take an inventory: What ideas have I adopted as true that should be re-examined and perhaps rejected?

> **ANY HEALTHY CHANGE IN OUR CHOICES AND CHARACTER BEGINS WITH DILIGENTLY CHANGING OUR MINDS.**

---WE PRAY---

"Christ, may my thoughts obey You today."

> BE ALERT AND OF SOBER MIND. YOUR ENEMY
> THE DEVIL PROWLS AROUND LIKE A ROARING LION
> LOOKING FOR SOMEONE TO DEVOUR.
> [1 PETER 5:8]

Nothing need rob us of the joy of the Lord and the winsomeness of new life in Him. However, it is also true that these are serious times and we are engaged in a serious struggle. When we allow ourselves to get distracted by temptation or comfortable with sin, we are inviting a lion into our lives to devour and destroy us completely. We must not let down our guard. This is what it means to be part of the Resistance.

Can you think of a time in your life or someone else's in which the devil was allowed to devour and things were never the same? Ask yourself: How can I stay "alert and of sober mind" today?

> **WE CAN'T AFFORD TO FORGET THAT AS DISCIPLES OF JESUS WE INDEED HAVE AN ENEMY WHOSE AIM IS OUR DEMISE.**

―― WE PRAY ――

"Lord, keep me alert to the traps and schemes of darkness."

> FINALLY, BE STRONG IN THE LORD
> AND IN HIS MIGHTY POWER. PUT ON THE
> FULL ARMOR OF GOD, SO THAT YOU CAN
> TAKE YOUR STAND AGAINST THE DEVIL'S SCHEMES.
> [EPHESIANS 6:10-11]

It's so important to remember we are fully equipped by the Lord to win our spiritual wars. Yes, our enemy schemes to trap us in temptation and ruin us if we let him, but we need not fall. In Christ, we can take our stand and must stand our ground. That is the Resistance.

This is not achieved in our own strength. We don't hold this line by only our white-knuckled effort. We take our meager willpower and apply it to strengthening ourselves in the Lord, putting on His full armor. Consider: On whose power do I most rely each day, my own or the Lord's through me?

> **IN CHRIST WE CAN BE FULLY EQUIPPED TO WIN OUR SPIRITUAL BATTLES AND POWERFULLY OVERCOME SIN.**

---WE PRAY---

"God, I choose to dress in Your armor today and stand on Your Word."

5
CONTROL YOURSELF

Keeping the Way means keeping it together. The Resistance we join has everything to do with the righteousness we pursue. So far we've learned that our first work is in ourselves, and that we must see through temptation and powerfully stand our spiritual ground. Now we come to realize **we can and should aim to become more and more like Christ.**

Let's be clear: Becoming a Christian absolutely sets us on a path toward becoming more and more like Christ and less and less like this world without Him. This truth is baked into the word *Christian*.

We don't do this on our own; the Holy Spirit enables us. However, neither is it something that magically happens to us without our cooperation. Sanctification is participatory, as Peter stated: "He has given us his very great and precious promises, so that through them you may participate in the divine nature, having escaped the corruption in the world caused by evil desires." (2 Peter 1:4) We have the opportunity to become more like our Creator, our True Father. Adopted into Christ, we now begin to inherit His likeness, His characteristics, and yes, His holiness. We finally get to escape the corrupting, downward pull of this world as it works in tandem with our selfish appetites.

This is a great summation of what we've been learning together so far. My goal is that we can be people who, having joined the Resistance, can move into the Rebellion and Revolution we'll discuss in our upcoming chapters. My prayer is that we would become mature and self-controlled, in possession of the strength of character and the credibility of lifestyle needed to humbly and bravely take a stand while lovingly and energetically changing the world. This is, to me, a compelling vision of what it really means to be a disciple of Jesus.

It was Leo Tolstoy who observed: "Everyone thinks of changing humanity, but no one thinks of changing himself."[1] This doesn't have to be true for us. Let's give our lives to change the world, no doubt. But let's also never stop the godly process of seeing ourselves changed. We're going to keep thinking about changing ourselves, or more accurately, how we partner with Christ to see ourselves changed, actually changed. How does this happen?

LIVE IN GRACE. IT NOT ONLY PARDONS US; IT EMPOWERS US.

Grace is the absolute foundation of our faith; it means as we live for Christ our sins no longer separate us from God, our Creator and Father. It's the "goodest" part of the Good News.

This is awesome, but it's just the beginning of all that grace does. As I touched on in Chapter Two, living each day in God's grace changes us. This is how Paul put it to Titus: "For the grace of God has appeared that offers salvation to all people." So far, so good; we get this. Grace offers salvation. But Paul goes on, "It teaches us to say 'No' to ungodliness and worldly passions, and to live self-controlled, upright and godly lives in this present age..." (Titus 2:11-12) This is the fullness of grace. It saves us *and* teaches us.

> **BECOMING A CHRISTIAN ABSOLUTELY SETS US ON A PATH TOWARD BECOMING MORE AND MORE LIKE CHRIST.**

This discipline of saying "no"—and learning what deserves our "no"—is the Resistance. We walk the Way and resist—say "no" to—all that would detour us. We see that grace equals, but is also greater than, forgiveness. Forgiveness is probably the first thing we think of when we consider grace, and rightly so. But we see in this passage that grace bestows upon us and develops in us self-control, uprightness, and godliness.

How does the grace "that offers salvation" also teach us to live "self-controlled, upright and godly lives in this present age"?

Grace turns the lights on, and we see just how deep a hole we were in. We come to understand where our life was heading with us in charge. As we experience the exhilaration that comes from being rescued—the adrenaline of the close call, the near miss—we shudder to realize how close we came to eternal death and a pointless life. We see we've been offered a second chance. We turn to the One extending to us this amazing grace, the One turning the lights on. He comes into focus and we stop, stunned.

We are now perceiving what and whom will be worthy of our devotion each and every day we have ahead: the Creator and Giver of life who chose to die and conquer death that we could fully live. Who and where we were without Him, and what He has done for us, comes into stark relief. We are humbled by the enormous cost of His sacrifice, the depth of our need—we were more desperate than we ever realized—and the distance He traversed to become one of us. We feel beneath us the solid ground of rightstanding before this holy God. A new Spirit fills us not only with joy but wisdom and discernment.

> **WE NEED TO LET GRACE SOAK INTO OUR CHARACTER, NOT JUST COVER OUR BEHAVIOR.**

That's how grace teaches us. It sheds light. It charges and changes us. It shows us the Way.

What I'm describing here is the difference between being a categorical Christian and a disciple of Jesus. Do we let grace merely forgive us, or do we let grace turn on the lights and teach us? The difference is profound. We need to let grace soak into our character, not just cover our behavior. Then you and I can look around in "this present age" and keep our heads, make good decisions, help others, control ourselves.

We will never be perfect this side of eternity. This bears repeating as we consider concepts like holiness and righteousness. Our judgment is flawed, we make mistakes, we're still healing from wounds, and still escaping the pulls of this world.

So in that sense we're always imperfect sinners. But we're now finally far from *only* that. Now, by God's grace, we can pay attention and tend to our hearts, from which everything we do flows. We can change what's going on in our hearts, pull the weeds that are choking God's Word in us, and cultivate the good God plants in us. In the most real way of all we get to exercise self-control. Our yes's and our no's are ours to say. We confess the sins we commit are a result of our conscious decisions, the courses of actions we choose. But now we can make new choices.

Now we can live in grace. It not only pardons us, it empowers us. It empowers us to choose holiness. We now have the ability to make a choice we never could have made before.

Choose holiness. We don't just experience Salvation; we engage in it.

God never removes our ability to choose. Even as we become Christians and are filled with His Spirit, we always get to choose, and are choosing all the time. We choose how we spend our day, the places we go, what we do and with whom we do it. And so we must accept responsibility for our Christlikeness, our spiritual health, our character growth. Again, salvation is a gift of grace—without question—but it is a robust, vibrant, purposeful gift that, once having received it, we get to engage with it.

If I give you the gift of a book, but you never read it, or clothes but you never wear them, or a car you never drive, or a trip you never take, you've barely—if at all in any real sense—*received* them. Certainly not for what they truly and fully are. The same is true of God's grace. It's so much more than something simply bestowed upon us; it's active and pervasive and does unique work in and through each of us as we receive it.

> **WE ACCEPT RESPONSIBILITY FOR OUR CHRISTLIKENESS, OUR SPIRITUAL HEALTH, OUR CHARACTER GROWTH.**

In Hebrews 12:14 we read: "Make every effort to live in peace with everyone and to be holy; without holiness no one will see the Lord." Wait a second…I thought I would "see the Lord" by God's grace. Yes, that's absolutely true. By grace through faith we are made holy and acceptable to God. But even that is a gift we receive *and* a life we then live. It's clothes we put on, a car we drive, a book we read. It's a Way we take and navigate.

Our responsibility to choose has not been taken away, but now a whole new set of choices has been made available to us. We can actually make some really healthy, wise decisions—consistently and wholeheartedly. More than that, we can actually experience holiness.

We choose holiness and become more like Christ when we engage in our salvation. Even though "you have been saved...not by works," you must also "continue to work out your salvation." (Ephesians 2:8-9 and Philippians 2:12) Remember, grace is opposed to earning, not to effort. We can get pretty sideways on that. It's never about maintaining good behavior so we can stay on God's good side, stay in His good graces. He loves us despite of, not because of, our behavior. And He does so passionately and relentlessly. But when we read in Hebrews that we are to "make every effort" (and we read this admonition multiple times in the New Testament), we begin to realize it's time to pedal this bicycle we've been given and follow the Way into God's good future for us. None of us will "be holy" by accident.

> **AS WE SEE THE BEAUTY OF CHRIST'S WAY, WE ALSO SEE THAT BY ITS VERY NATURE IT EXCLUDES SOME OTHER LESSER WAYS OF LIVING.**

So what does such choosing, such effort, look like? It includes at least two practices: limiting our options and disciplining our bodies.

Keeping to the Way means we cut off all divergent paths. As we see the beauty of Christ's Way, we also see that by its very nature it excludes some other ways of life and lesser living. We see certain decisions we've made and actions we've taken in the past now simply no longer fit. We close off those paths when we choose this Way. Indeed they have lost—or are quickly losing—their appeal.

In short, we don't keep your options open, which is something we all in our humanness can be tempted to do. In the thick of all this talk of holiness and keeping to the Way we might say (if not out loud, then in our deeper thoughts and motives), "Y'know, Rob, that's great, but grace forgives me. And every now and then Friday night rolls around, and I kinda like to have my options open."

But with our hearts—our actual will and sincere intentions—we begin to see the beauty of God's way of living. (Remember, grace turns the lights on.) And while we know we'll never be perfect at it, we do decide to intelligently and strategically plan to keep to this Way. And get right back on it when we stray. It is essential that this becomes true of us. But is it?

Or do we sort of keep one door open? Do we say to ourselves, "Well...I'm thinking about leaving the Way a little bit next weekend, but I know grace covers that."? Our answers speak to our intention. Is sin something we avoid because we see it as the deadly cancer to our souls it is? Or is sin something we agree we should generally do less of and not more of, but y'know...when the right opportunity comes around there's always at least a little we've kept in our back pocket? I cannot overstate how pivotal this distinction is for anyone seeking to not wreck his or her life.

> **OUR CHRISTIAN FAITH IS NOT JUST A BELIEF WE HOLD, IT IS A BELIEF THAT HOLDS US.**

When we see the excellence of this ancient Way, we're not constantly remaking the decision, re-answering the question in its various forms: Am I going to leave the Way? Am I going to choose to do that for which I know I'll ask forgiveness later? It means cutting off disparate paths and closing useless, misleading doors. Certain conclusions are now simply "no."

It also means realizing our bodies and what we do with them are actually among our most spiritual possessions and decisions.

Paul wrote to the Thessalonians: "Each of you should learn to control your own body in a way that is holy and honorable..." (1 Thessalonians 4:4). We just read earlier that grace *teaches* us, and now we're being told to *learn*. Learn what? Self-control, specifically regarding our bodies. Clearly, this reinforces the importance and necessity of our engagement. We rarely, if ever, learn anything truly or deeply by accident or against our will.

Here we are being exhorted to "learn to control your own body in a way that is holy and honorable." What I do, whatever I do, I do with my body. Where these feet take me, what and whom my hands touch, what my eyes see...these are choices I make with my body. Dallas Willard put it like this in his book, *Revolution of Character*: "The way of Christ is relentlessly incarnational—it is *bodily*. ...Our body is an essential part of who we are, and no redemption that omits it is full redemption."[2] In other words, we live in these bodies. What we do with our bodies is what we're doing with our lives. The Christian faith is about real life, our day-to-day actions and decisions. It's not just a belief we hold, it is a belief that holds us.

This theme is a recurring one in Scripture. "Therefore, I urge you, brothers and sisters, in view of God's mercy, to offer your bodies as a living sacrifice, holy and pleasing to God—this is your true and proper worship." (Romans 12:1) Again, we don't let go of grace and mercy; in fact, it's "in view of God's mercy" that we surrender our bodies to holiness.

We're squarely seeing here the idea of self-discipline and self-control, which is, of course, at the heart of joining the Resistance. We live out this Resistance and this pursuit of holiness most readily through spiritual disciplines.

There are spiritual disciplines of engagement: prayer, meditating on Scripture, service, and giving, to name a few. And then there are disciplines of abstinence, like fasting, silence, and solitude. In these disciplines we learn to deny ourselves in things that don't seriously matter, so we can be ready and primed to deny ourselves in things that do. We abstain to some degree and for some time from the satisfaction of normal desires in order to develop self-control.

> **IN TODAY'S SOCIETY WE'VE DISTORTED WHAT FREEDOM MEANS AND REJECTED ANYTHING THAT PROPOSES TO DENY OUR APPETITES THEIR FULFILLMENT.**

Keep in mind, such desires aren't wrong. But in today's society we've distorted what freedom means and rejected anything that proposes to deny our appetites their fulfillment. If we don't find control over our appetites—a control most fully and rightly found in Christ—then our appetites will surely control us. Many of life's tragedies stem from this fact.

If we spend our lives never learning to deny ourselves (even of inconsequential things), what makes us think we will suddenly be able to do so when the consequences are high and we must? When failing to do so can be ruinous? It's a fact: If our self-control is underdeveloped, we will in all likelihood fall for temptation. And not just once or once in a while.

Bible teacher Beth Moore writes, "Any person without self-control is either an accident looking for a place to happen or a slave in chains. ...We are desperate for self-control, and in its absence, we are drowning in self-defeat."³ She's right. And it's interesting: When we retain authority over our lives we actually lack the self-control we need to keep them healthy. It's only as we relinquish "lordship" of our lives to Christ that we can cultivate—by His presence in us—the self-control we desperately need. It is a fruit of the Spirit (see Galatians 5:22-23). It's a virtue that grows in us because we are filled with and continually open to the Holy Spirit.

> **SELFISHNESS IS OUR DEFAULT SETTING AS HUMAN BEINGS, BUT IN CHRIST WE CAN BE REWIRED.**

Jesus was the epitome of self-control, and we can be like Him by living in not only the pardon but the power of grace, by not only experiencing salvation but engaging in it, and by finding freedom not only from sin but from our very selves.

Pledge your allegiance. If Christ is not King, we are slaves to our selves.

Slaves to our selves. This is not a good thing to be.

Bible scholar William Barclay once wrote, "The tragedy of life and of the world is not that men do not know God; the tragedy is that, knowing Him, they still insist on going their own way."⁴ There it is, where it all comes to a point: His Way or my way, keeping to His wise and beautiful Way or sticking with my own. Servants of "our Great God and Savior, Jesus Christ" (see Titus 2:13) or slaves to our selves? It's a choice we all make. One we make every day.

Paul said of himself, "I discipline my body and keep it under control, lest after preaching to others I myself should be disqualified." (1 Corinthians 9:27 ESV) and that "those who belong to Christ Jesus have crucified the flesh with its passions and desires." (Galatians 5:24) In other words, we subject our body to *our will to follow God's will* and don't make ourselves subject to our body's appetites and wants.

Paul said this because he knew selfishness is our default setting as human beings. But in Christ we can be rewired. So we put to death—we starve to death—the selfishness in us, the self-centeredness which is indeed the heart of the problem for us all.

Consider the following study, which I find fascinating. In 1948, psychologists asked more than 10,000 adolescents whether they considered themselves to be a very important person. At that point, 12 percent said yes. The same question was asked of adolescents in 2003, and it was 80 percent who answered, "Yes, I am a very important person."[5] Perhaps we've all just developed a better self-esteem. Or perhaps there's more to it than that.

According to New York Times columnist David Brooks in his book, *The Road to Character*, psychologists have a diagnostic called the narcissism test. Narcissism is defined as "excessive or erotic interest in oneself, extreme self-centeredness." Subjects of this test are asked whether given statements apply to them. Statements such as, "I like to be the center of attention" and "I show off if I get the chance because I am extraordinary" and "Somebody should write a biography about me." The more you and I agree with such statements, the more narcissistic we are.

The median narcissism score has risen 30 percent in the last two decades. Ninety-three percent of young people score higher than what was the middle score just twenty years ago. Along with this, there has been, according to Brooks, a tremendous increase in the desire for fame. In a 1976 survey that asked people to list their life goals, fame ranked fifteenth out of sixteen. By 2007, 51 percent of young people reported that being famous was one of their top personal goals.[6]

> **WE ARE BECOMING A CULTURE OF PEOPLE WHO BELIEVE—ALMOST WITHOUT EXAGGERATION OR METAPHOR—THE WORLD REALLY DOES REVOLVE AROUND US, OR THAT AT LEAST IT SHOULD.**

In short, as a culture we are becoming people who increasingly believe—almost without exaggeration or metaphor—the world really does revolve around us, or that at least it should. Tim Keller diagnoses this well:

> Instead of trying to shape our desires to fit reality, we now seek to control and shape reality to fit our desires. The ancients looked at an anxious person and prescribed *spiritual character change*. Modernity talks instead about stress-management techniques.[7] (*emphasis* mine)

In other words, as a whole, our motivation to change the world as human beings and as a society is to make it more like what we want, so we don't have to change ourselves. Keepers of the Way see through this. We see it in ourselves, no doubt, but we see past it.

Self-control is not a limitation of our freedoms. It is a discovery of them. We are free from the tyranny of our fickle and relentless appetites, free from falling for temptation's lies and falling into sin's traps, free from the pressure to be like everyone else and instead free to be like Christ.

In our surrender to God's will we are not giving up our will, erasing it or denying it. Really we are finally employing it as it was designed to be: in submission to and in concert with our Creator. We are willing God's will to be made real in our living. In his book, *Renovation of the Heart*, Dallas Willard describes our surrender: "It is for the first time to have a will that is fully functional, not at war with itself, and capable of directing all of the parts of the self in harmony with one another under the direction of God."[8]

Apart from and without Christ we are in every way truly *self-centered*. We can't help it. And with our selves at our centers, our souls and psyches become black holes, insatiable vacuums void of eternal significance. But no more. The Way of Jesus, of the Resistance, lifts us from this pull and re-centers us, putting us not at the axis of meaning—we were never meant for that—but in orbit around the One who never leaves, never lies, never ends.

As I conclude this chapter and this section about joining the Resistance, I want to turn our attention to this powerful passage of Scripture which not only summarizes what we've been learning so far, but speaks to what we'll begin covering next. Peter by the Holy Spirit says it so much better than I can.

> Therefore, since Christ suffered in his body, arm yourselves also with the same attitude, because whoever suffers in the body is done with sin. As a result, they do not live the rest of their earthly lives for evil human desires, but rather for the will of God. For you have spent

enough time in the past doing what pagans choose to do—living in debauchery, lust, drunkenness, orgies, carousing and detestable idolatry. They are surprised that you do not join them in their reckless, wild living, and they heap abuse on you. But they will have to give account to him who is ready to judge the living and the dead. (1 Peter 4:1-5)

> HE HAS GIVEN US HIS VERY GREAT AND PRECIOUS
> PROMISES, SO THAT THROUGH THEM YOU
> MAY PARTICIPATE IN THE DIVINE NATURE,
> HAVING ESCAPED THE CORRUPTION IN THE WORLD
> CAUSED BY EVIL DESIRES.
> [2 PETER 1:4]

The Resistance isn't only about not falling into temptation or fighting just to hold our ground. It's this and so much more. It's ultimately about keeping ourselves in a position in which we can become more and more like Jesus. Through Him we escape corruption and are freed from the tyranny of our lower natures. We can now "participate in the divine nature" and become the person God designed us to be, the one He had in mind from our beginning.

God longs to keep His promises. Contemplate God's promises to you and ask: How can I become more like Christ? How can I keep God's promises to me?

THE GOOD PROMISES OF GOD EXPRESSED IN CHRIST MAKE IT POSSIBLE FOR US TO ACTUALLY BE MORE LIKE HIM.

—— WE PRAY ——

"Holy Father, thank You for keeping Your promise to make me like You."

THE GRACE OF GOD...TEACHES US TO SAY "NO" TO UNGODLINESS AND WORLDLY PASSIONS, AND TO LIVE SELF-CONTROLLED, UPRIGHT AND GODLY LIVES IN THIS PRESENT AGE...
[TITUS 2:11-12]

There is a huge difference between righteousness and self-righteousness, between holiness and having a "holier-than-thou" attitude. Being part of the Resistance means living a godly life while understanding this doesn't make us morally superior to others, but spiritually empowered by God's grace. As Dallas Willard has written, disciples of Jesus pursuing godliness consume grace like a 747 burns jet fuel at takeoff.

Think it through: Do I realistically consider myself as having the God-given potential to master my passions and live righteously?

> **GOD'S GRACE NOT ONLY FORGIVES OUR SIN, BUT EMPOWERS US TO SIN LESS AND LIVE RIGHTEOUSLY.**

---WE PRAY---

"God, teach me when to say 'yes' and when to say 'no'."

Each of you should learn to control your own body in a way that is holy and honorable…
[1 Thessalonians 4:4]

Scripture doesn't allow us to keep theological truths as only theoretical. Theology—thinking about the truth and reality of God—is always practical. And this material, natural world is not to be seen as irrelevant to the supernatural realm. Everything is spiritual, including and especially our physical bodies.

As Christians, our body houses our spirit (our true self) as well as the Holy Spirit. So what we do with our body is an expression of our spirit—who we really are. Where our feet take us, who and what we touch with our hands, on what we focus our eyes…all of this is our body doing as our spirit directs. Ask yourself: To what degree do I consider the spiritual implications of my physical desires and actions?

WHAT WE DO WITH OUR BODIES IS NOT UNSPIRITUAL, BUT A PRIMARY EXPRESSION OF OUR DEVOTION TO JESUS.

—WE PRAY—

"Spirit, teach me to control my body and its appetites so that I honor You."

IN YOUR STRUGGLE AGAINST SIN, YOU HAVE NOT YET RESISTED TO THE POINT OF SHEDDING YOUR BLOOD.
[HEBREWS 12:4]

It's easy for any of us to begin to slack in our Resistance, gradually underestimating what's at stake. Our sins become mere "mistakes" and we become less concerned with displeasing God and more with the consequences of getting caught. But this, of course, is our common delusion. Don't be fooled: the results of such negligence can be fatal. Our Spirit-reliant self-discipline is like chemotherapy to the cancer of sin.

Disciples of Jesus "have crucified the flesh with its passions and desires." (Galatians 5:24) Reckon with it: When it comes to my struggle against sin, how much fight is in me?

> **SIN AND ITS CONSEQUENCES CANNOT BE TAKEN CASUALLY, NOT IN OURSELVES, NOT IN OTHERS, NOT IN THIS WORLD.**

---WE PRAY---

"Father, help me fight the good fight of faith with everything I am."

> ALL OF US, THEN, WHO ARE MATURE SHOULD TAKE SUCH A VIEW OF THINGS. AND IF ON SOME POINT YOU THINK DIFFERENTLY, THAT TOO GOD WILL MAKE CLEAR TO YOU. ONLY LET US LIVE UP TO WHAT WE HAVE ALREADY ATTAINED.
> [PHILIPPIANS 3:15-16]

As we've already considered, keeping up the Resistance includes not giving back to the enemy the ground we've struggled to win. This dynamic applies especially to our thoughts, our beliefs, and our worldwiew. Returning to former ways of thinking is a precursor to returning to former ways of living. Cynicism, doubt, and intellectual pride can all seduce us into questioning our faith and reducing our resistance.

Consider how the tiniest false idea can take root and upheave even the firmest faith and ask: Am I too easily slipping back into immature thinking?

> **A SIGNIFICANT PART OF PROGRESSING IN OUR WALK WITH CHRIST IS NO LONGER REGRESSING AS WE USED TO.**

—WE PRAY—

"God, correct me where I'm wrong and keep me right in You."

> FOR THOUGH WE LIVE IN THE WORLD,
> WE DO NOT WAGE WAR AS THE WORLD DOES.
> [2 CORINTHIANS 10:3]

Jesus said His way will always be the one less traveled because so many either neglect or reject it. Our Resistance rarely makes sense to those who don't yet know Jesus. Discipleship can seem restrictive while worldliness can seem so attractive. This is how our resistance inevitably fosters our rebellion against this world and its ways. We see that we're never merely standing our ground; we're also standing out and going against the flow.

Contemplate this dynamic: The more I become like Jesus, the less I fit in with society-at-large. Am I ready to be a humble renegade for Him?

> **OUR ACTS OF OBEDIENCE TO GOD CAN CONCURRENTLY BE ACTS OF CIVIL DISOBEDIENCE TO THE WAYS OF THIS WORLD.**

---WE PRAY---

"Lord, give me Your wisdom to help me choose my battles."

FUEL THE REBELLION

Do not be conformed to this world
[Romans 12:2]

6
DEFY EXPECTATIONS

I'd like review two of the observations I made in Chapter One regarding certain forces or realities we see in effect all around us today, ones that can keep us from keeping the Way.

First, Christianity has been around for a long time now and familiarity has bred contempt, or at least boredom and cynicism. The prevalence, even historical dominance, of Christianity is making it easier to reject in a world fascinated by the new. But I hope you can see that the Way of Jesus, though ancient, remains right and good in every respect. Christians have always been pilgrims. This is the subject of part one: Join the Resistance.

Secondly, some Christians in the public sphere are a tragic misrepresentation and even embarrassment. As a result, we may find ourselves hedging our identification with Christianity. As we begin Part Two of this book, we will see that we mustn't step away from identifying with Christ, but instead learn what that truly means. Christians have always been non-conformists, which is the subject of this next section, Fuel the Rebellion.

I recently read again about how when Rome was at the height of glory and power, our disturbing sect entered the scene. These "Christians" didn't fall in line, but dared to be different no matter the cost. In an era when immorality, lavishness, and luxury were celebrated, Christians refused to be defiled by the sensual practices of a disintegrating civilization. When human life was cheapened, they highly valued human beings, their souls and destinies.

These Christians refused to be absorbed into the godless society of Rome. They had not heard of the rule we hear today: "When in Rome, do as the Romans do." The Roman government initiated a drive to stamp out Christianity as a disturber of the peace. All had to bow to Caesar, to conform to pagan custom, and to behave like true Romans. Nonconformists were threatened with death, and many chose death rather than comply to Rome's demands and compromise their convictions.

Are Christians today any different? We shouldn't be. **We must no longer shrink ourselves to fit in with this world. It's not worth it.**

We keep returning to Jesus' visual of the broad road that most people choose and unwittingly follow to destruction, as well as its off ramp, the narrow Way that leads to life. This word picture comes into sharp focus as we transition from joining the Resistance and humbly standing our ground to fueling the Rebellion and inevitably going against the flow of the world.

As we move ahead, it's essential we understand the concept of "the world" we encounter throughout the New Testament. What did the biblical authors mean by this term? "The world" (*kosmos* in the Greek) is human society and culture without God, without truth. This world—to which we all belonged before Christ and in which we still live—may often be well-intentioned, but remains incomplete in what it knows and can do. It is by its nature ignorant of God's truth and unable to tap His power. On a personal level, "the world" is anything that makes temptation look good and sin appear normal.

> "THE WORLD" IS ANYTHING THAT MAKES TEMPTATION LOOK GOOD AND SIN APPEAR NORMAL.

Christ and His Way stand in contrast to the world. And we stand for one or the other in at least the following three ways.

What molds our character? We conform to one or the other.

It was Paul the Roman Christian who wrote this word to his fellow believing citizens and for all Christians of all times: "Do not conform to the pattern of this world, but be transformed by the renewing of your mind." (Romans 12:2)

DEFY EXPECTATIONS

There's a mold, a pattern to life without God. It's predictable and monotonous. It works hard to perennially dress itself up as original and attractive, but it's the same rehashed recipe of money and stuff, pleasure and comfort, power and glory. Even though relatively few people actually get much of any of these things at all or for long, the masses of this world will keep chasing them, keep falling for them—perhaps spending their whole lives doing so. It's the pattern of the world. And if we don't rebel against its pressure and pull with a power not of this world, we will find ourselves conforming to it.

I remember my rebellious phase as a teenager. It mostly manifested itself in a bad attitude and just generally acting like a punk. My rebellion didn't count for anything. It was immature and mostly about the clothes I wore and the music I listened to. This kind of clichéd rebellion didn't achieve anything and eventually I grew out of it. But there is something to be said for that rebellious edge and energy.

> **TRANSFORMATION IS THE TRUEST REBELLION. COMFORTABLE CONFORMITY IS OVERRATED.**

I'm not so sure growing out of that intensity entirely is always best. I think too often what we pass off as maturity is really apathy and lethargy.

Worthwhile rebellion comes from believing we now see the world differently, perhaps seeing what most others don't, or seeing through what most others fall for. That can be good. When it ripens, such rebellion can be world-changing. Christians can be—should be—rebels with a cause. I believe Christianity offers us a chance to rebel in ways that actually mean something and make a substantive difference. Transformation is the truest rebellion. Comfortable conformity is overrated. Maybe the world could use a few more Jesus-followers with a rebellious, non-conformist edge. Maybe the Church could, too.

Here's the dynamic at play: Without God, we conform to the world; with Him, we can conform to Christ. "For those God foreknew" (that's all of us), "he also predestined to be conformed to the image of his Son." (Romans 8:29) In other words, when we give God room to work in our lives, He always grows us toward being more like Jesus, the prototypical human, the embodiment of what God wants for each of us, His destiny for us. If we don't give God such a workspace in our souls, the world will fill the void. John reminds us, "For everything in the world—the lust of the flesh, the lust of the eyes, and the pride of life—comes not from the Father but from the world." (1 John 2:16)

We all draw from one of two sources. The Father aims us toward Christ and Christlikeness. Jesus is expansive. Jesus is never-ending. Jesus is wise and brilliant and all good. We can spend our entire lives learning from Him and seeking to emulate Him and never find the end of His inspiration and example. We can grow and grow and grow. But what comes from the world aims us toward ourselves, enclosing us upon ourselves. The mold and pattern of this world is very small and limited, so very confined and confining.

Reflecting on Romans 12:2 and the circumstances of its original readers and of Christians today, Billy Graham has observed:

> Times have changed, but human nature hasn't. The pagan world is still trying to put its stamp of conformity on every follower of Jesus Christ. Every possible pressure is being brought to bear upon Christians to make them conform to the standards of the world. In our desire to make Christ known and to increase the influence of the church, we are prone to think that Christians and the church can be made popular with the unbelieving world. This is a grave mistake.[1]

In order to spread the message of Jesus more widely, we may be tempted to knock off a few of its edges concerning sin and repentance, or to smooth out those rough places regarding self-denial and holiness. We may want to make the life of a disciple more palatable, even popular. But, of course, popularity mustn't be our goal, but rather honesty. The Gospel is good stuff. This is life-giving, life-changing truth we receive from Jesus. Let's just live it and share it. Thoughtful in our methods, to be sure, but sincere and transparent in our message. It's the only real way we'll make it heard and understood, for far too many reject the message only because they've never truly heard it.

> **POPULARITY MUSTN'T BE OUR GOAL, BUT RATHER HONESTY. THE GOSPEL IS GOOD STUFF. WE SIMPLY LIVE IT AND SHARE IT.**

Much has been made of the rise of the "nones," that category of Americans who answer Pew Research's surveys with "none" when asked about their religious affiliation. In 2014, they found that 23 percent of Americans self-identified in this way—a seven-point jump in as many years.[2]

I recently saw what I think is a cogent and profound way to interpret this finding. It's illustrated in a webcomic by Adam Ford. The scene is easy for me to describe to you: Three people stand in the frame, each wearing a t-shirt that identifies their stance. "Non-Christian" on one side and "Christian" facing him in conversation from the other side, with "Meh" standing between them.

> America 20 Years Ago…
>> Non-Christian: *"I am definitely not a Christian."*
>> Christian: *"I am definitely a Christian."*
>> Meh (standing next to Christian): *"I honestly don't care that much about following Jesus, but it's socially advantageous for me to self-identify as a Christian. So that's what I do."*
>
> America Today…
>> Non-Christian: *"I am definitely not a Christian."*
>> Christian: *"I am definitely a Christian."*
>> Meh (has moved to stand next to Non-Christian): *"Ok, so times have changed and it's no longer socially advantageous for me to self-identify as a Christian. So I stopped. I'm on this side now."*
>
> What the Headlines Say…
>> Non-Christian: *"Dang, Christian. Pew Research says you're dying over there. There used to be two of you and now there's only one. You should be worried."*
>
> What the Truth Is…
>> Christian: *"Nah. There was really only one of me before and there's still one of me. The 'Meh' guy just got more honest. And oddly enough… I feel healthier than I have in a long time."*[3]

The headlines may make us think the Church's days are waning, as if we're on the wrong side of history or behind the curve. But perhaps we're just entering a time in which people are being more honest. We can be honest as well, and lots of good things can flow from that.

So as truth and morality are up for grabs in this world, we must choose to let our character conform to an unchanging, perfect Christ and not an ever-changing, fickle world. We can humbly and steadfastly stand and simply say: "I am a Christian. This is who I am."

I believe down to my toes these thoughts of Dallas Willard in his book, *The Great Omission*, are profoundly true:

> The greatest issue facing the world today, with all its heartbreaking needs, is whether those who, by profession or culture, are identified as "Christians" will become disciples—students, apprentices, practitioners—of Jesus Christ, steadily learning from him how to live the life of the Kingdom of the Heavens into every corner of human existence.[4]

In the end the greatest issue—the only thing that can turn the tide of our society, what will define how this era of history will be understood—is whether those who call themselves Christians will indeed embody all that title means and determine to live as disciples of Jesus. Categories won't define us; survey answers no longer matter, if they ever did. The stakes have risen and the time for candor has arrived. Who are we going to be in this generation, in this world? Who and what will we allow to mold our character?

> **THE STAKES HAVE RISEN. THE TIME FOR CANDOR HAS ARRIVED. WHO ARE WE GOING TO BE IN THE GENERATION, IN THIS WORLD?**

What captures our hearts? We love one or the other.

What fills our hearts leads our lives. What we love, what brings us joy, says a lot about who we are and the direction we're going. Religious writers of earlier generations used to call these our "affections." It's only natural that whatever captures our affections occupies our thoughts, drives our decisions, and fills our speech. We will spend our time and money on what we care about most. That's why we absolutely must ask ourselves: What has captivated and filled my heart?

John the Apostle said with the precision and clarity of a mathematical proof, "Do not love the world or anything in the world. If anyone loves the world, love for the Father is not in them." (1 John 2:15) Again, we read the dichotomy between this world system and life in Christ.

Fueling the Rebellion means checking ourselves: If I am perfectly at home and comfortable in a godless culture, what does that say about the culture of my soul and heart? You see, the world vies for our affections, wants to enamor us with its descriptions of success and promises of fulfillment. God knows this. And like a faithful spouse, He longs to see us remain faithful to Him. James paints the picture even more starkly than John: "You adulterous people, don't you know that friendship with the world means enmity against God? Therefore, anyone who chooses to be a friend of the world becomes an enemy of God." (James 4:4) You're getting confused, James says. You want to be popular in society, successful by this world's empty standards. Quit thinking there's such a thing as two-timing God.

> IF I AM PERFECTLY AT HOME IN A GODLESS CULTURE, WHAT DOES THAT SAY ABOUT THE CULTURE OF MY SOUL?

To long to be loved within society, to need its acceptance, is to say God's love and acceptance aren't enough for us. To fill our hearts with affection for what this world says is important is to miss the point of God's sacrificial devotion, indeed to dishonor the passion of His love for us and to leave the Way. And yet, how badly we can want to be "a friend of the world" as James puts it. To be liked, applauded, esteemed, admired. Hear this wisdom from Hannah More, an abolitionist, poet, and reformer who worked alongside William Wilberforce to abolish slavery in the British Empire:

> The woman who derives her principles from the Bible...will not pant for beholders. She is no clamorous beggar for the extorted alms of admiration. She lives on her own stock. She possesses the

truest independence. She does not wait for the opinion of the world to know if she is right; nor for the applause of the world, to know if she is happy.[5]

How accurate and inspiring she was and her words are. Her advice is useful for us all. Hers is the voice of a rebel. The number of likes on her latest Facebook post or how often she's re-tweeted would not have determined her sense of worth or wellbeing. She was a courageous non-conformist in multiple ways. She paid a price for it. She beat the system. She changed the world.

Few things keep us more tethered to this world than the opinions of others and the importance we place on them. And while, of course, there's nothing intrinsically wrong with being well-regarded by others, it too easily can become a driver of our lives. But something happens when we become a disciple of Jesus: We're untethered, freed from this tyranny. As we mature, we find that whether it be praise or criticism from others, we learn what we can from them and then let both roll off our shoulders and find no residence in our hearts. The applause of this world fades into irrelevance as we stay focused on the only One whose approval matters. As nineteenth century Scottish pastor Thomas Chalmers wrote: "Christians overcome the world by seeing the beauty and excellence of Christ. They overcome the world by seeing something more attractive than the world: Christ."[6]

> **THE APPLAUSE OF THIS WORLD FADES INTO IRRELEVANCE AS WE STAY FOCUSED ON THE ONLY ONE WHOSE APPROVAL MATTERS.**

Speaking of defying expectations, let me take this opportunity which Hannah More affords me to make an observation—perhaps as an aside to our main topic, perhaps not.

People don't much know who Hannah More was, but they know her comrade William Wilberforce. This reveals something worth our attention. Tragically, much of the Church over much of our history has been "expected" to be male dominated and—in ways both subtle and overt—to suppress women or see them as less gifted in leadership or insight. This is a sad and misplaced expectation we should defy.

For all its boasting to the contrary, our world is far from healthy in this regard. Just one small example would be the gender wage gap of 21 percent in our country. And this is to say nothing of the way women are treated in other countries or by the dictates of other faiths.

I believe strongly that the Church can defy expectations, take the lead, and outpace the world in honoring and empowering our daughters, sisters, wives, and mothers to become all God designed them to be. The world doesn't have this right. We can do better.

What guides our lives? We gain and lose one or the other.

We've been discussing worldliness and must be clear about what it means. Worldliness is less about refraining from certain practices or avoiding certain places, and more about what's forming our worldview. When are we being or becoming worldly? When we let the world inform our identity, our ethic, our aspirations, we are becoming worldly. Many things in this world can be enjoyed when kept in perspective, but when we let a worldview that ignores or defies God influence our POV on what's true and false, right and wrong, we are becoming worldly.

In other words, what sets our aim and guides our life? To what and for what are we giving our soul? This is the way

> **IT'S A POOR TRADE-OFF. WE CAN WHITTLE DOWN OUR VERY SOULS BY STRAINING TO GAIN MORE AND MORE IN THIS WORLD.**

Jesus put it: "What good will it be for someone to gain the whole world, yet forfeit their soul? Or what can anyone give in exchange for their soul?" (Matthew 16:26) He knows there's a trade-off we're always making. And we can whittle down our very souls by straining to gain more and more in this world. The returns are ever-diminishing and ultimately disappointing.

Many of us today can suffer from what has been cheekily labeled FOMO: the Fear Of Missing Out. On its surface, FOMO seeks to explain why we seemingly can't go more than a minute or two without thumbing our phones and checking our social media feeds. The stream of photos and status updates and tweets and live videos never stops and we fear missing something "important." But FOMO has always been around. As is true of so much, the Internet only amplifies it. Spiritually speaking, we humans have fallen for FOMO anytime we've wondered if the exchange of our old life and old ways for new life in Christ and His Way would leave us wanting, missing out on something we'd regret giving up.

But anyone who follows through on following Jesus discovers we gain incomparably more than we "lose." The exchange is always worth it. As Paul famously declared, "I consider everything a loss because of the surpassing worth of knowing Christ Jesus my Lord, for whose sake I have lost all things. I consider them garbage, that I may gain Christ." (Philippians 3:8) When Peter began to suffer a brief bout of FOMO and inquired of Jesus, "We have left everything to follow you! What then will there be for us?" Jesus promised: "Everyone who has left houses or brothers or sisters or father or mother or wife or children or fields for my sake will receive a hundred times as much and will inherit eternal life." (Matthew 19:27-29)

In the Garden, the devil tricked Adam and Eve into trading their devoted obedience to God for some pretty disappointing knowledge of good and evil. Their FOMO got the better of them, to say the least. But this was only the beginning. During Jesus' forty days of fasting and consecration before launching His ministry, Satan tempted Him with an exchange by showing Him "all the kingdoms of the world and their splendor. 'All this I will give you,' he said, 'if you will bow down and worship me.'" (Matthew 4:8-9) Fortunately, Jesus knew the score and refused to be deceived.

> **WHEN WE FOLLOW THROUGH ON FOLLOWING JESUS WE DISCOVER WE GAIN INCOMPARABLY MORE THAN WE "LOSE."**

The devil was trying to make a deal. He's always trying to make such a deal...with you, me, everyone. And everyone has a choice to make. As a whole, humankind has consistently failed in this. Paul describes the transaction in epic terms. And he's not only describing idol-crafting pagans from some dark age, but our "enlightened" era is equally well-represented:

> Although they claimed to be wise, they became fools and exchanged the glory of the immortal God for images made to look like a mortal human being and birds and animals and reptiles. ...They exchanged the truth about God for a lie, and worshiped and served created things rather than the Creator—who is forever praised. (Romans 1:22-25)

Here's the raw deal we humans keep falling for: We exchange the glory of the immortal God whom we can't always understand and can never control for images and things we can understand and control. The mystery and wonder—and yes, holiness—of the Creator for the earthiness, the predictability, the immediacy of what He's created (or we've created).

It's easier to have idols we pretend can guide us, substitutes for the real thing that don't hold us accountable, but give us enough of an emotional/psychological kick we can feel good about them and ourselves. But keepers of the Way can rob the pagan temples of this world, so to speak, and set a different example. We can reject the system that defines people by their wealth, their looks, or their power. (What a joke and a lie. Wealth is temporary, looks can't last, and power is a prideful illusion.) We can refuse to agree with the morality the world approves. As Bible teacher Beth Moore says: "Sin makes you stupid."[7] It impairs your judgment, seemingly knocking off IQ points. We see this all around us. But God wants to give us wisdom to make good decisions, stringing such decisions together to form a healthy, wise life. How? By choosing His truth and setting our minds on it.

> **WE CAN ROB THE PAGAN TEMPLES OF THIS WORLD, SO TO SPEAK, AND SET A DIFFERENT EXAMPLE.**

This is another way Scripture frames the exchange: the wisdom of the world or the wisdom of God. Which worldview will win? Which wisdom will we make our own? On which will we set our minds? *Mindset* is defined as "the ideas and attitudes with which a person approaches a situation, habits of mind formed by previous experiences, a fixed mental disposition that predetermines a person's responses and choices."[8]

We must set our minds on the Way, the Truth, and the Life (see John 14:6). We let His teaching shape our thoughts because our thoughts shape us. The importance of our chosen mindset is reinforced repeatedly in the New Testament and is as real and insightful as any psychological theory or diagnosis...

Set your minds on things above, not on earthly things. (Colossians 3:2)

Those who live according to the flesh have their minds set on what the flesh desires; but those who live in accordance with the Spirit have their minds set on what the Spirit desires. The mind governed by the flesh is death, but the mind governed by the Spirit is life and peace. (Romans 8:5-6)

> **THE EARLY CHURCH NEVER LOOKED TO THE GOVERNMENT FOR GUIDANCE. WE DON'T CONSULT THE CULTURE TO DETERMINE OUR CONVICTIONS.**

For, as I have often told you before and now tell you again even with tears, many live as enemies of the cross of Christ. Their destiny is destruction, their god is their stomach, and their glory is in their shame. Their mind is set on earthly things. But our citizenship is in heaven. And we eagerly await a Savior from there, the Lord Jesus Christ, (Philippians 3:18-20)

Think about it. A lie doesn't become truth, wrong doesn't become right, and evil doesn't become good because it's accepted by the majority, promoted by the media, or funded by the state. The early church never looked to the government for guidance. As Chesterton once said, "Fallacies do not cease to be fallacies because they become fashions."[9] We don't consult the culture to determine our convictions.

Jesus says we have another source: "...the Spirit of truth. The world cannot accept him, because it neither sees him nor knows him. But you know him, for he lives with you and will be in you." (John 14:17) The world cannot accept Him. We see that everyday. This One the world cannot accept lives in us. He is our guide. This is the very essence of our Rebellion. The empire of Caesar holds no promise—and carries no intimidation—for the citizens of the Kingdom of Jesus.

To quote G.K. Chesterton once more: "A dead thing goes with the stream but only a living thing can go against it."[10] Friend, our faith in Christ is a living thing. And I pray that your faith is a vibrant, living thing inside you, kicking against the ways of this world with energy and stamina, going against the flow. I pray you don't forget that this world wants to take that vigorous and vital faith and shove it, mold it, suffocate it, and kill it.

In October 2015, some students at Oregon's Umpqua Community College lived or died based on their answer to a gunman's question, "Are you a Christian?"[11] In a less urgent but no less real way, the world is asking you and me that question every day.

We have choices to make and we're making them now, today, everyday: Who am I? What do I stand for? Am I a Christian, a disciple of Jesus?

When it comes to Jesus and this world, who or what molds our character? Captures our hearts? Guides our lives? We conform to one or the other. We love one or the other. We gain and lose one or the other

I ask again: Are Christians today any different than those of the first century? We shouldn't be. So let's follow their example and not shrink ourselves to fit in with this world. It's not worth it.

DO NOT CONFORM TO THE PATTERN OF THIS WORLD, BUT BE TRANSFORMED BY THE RENEWING OF YOUR MIND.
[ROMANS 12:2]

Peer pressure and the compulsion to conform aren't always things we leave behind in adolescence. The pressure may become more subtle, but it's no less pervasive. Left to ourselves, that pressure too often prevails and we unthinkingly follow the pattern of this world. And the pattern doesn't ever truly change: looks, wealth, success, fame... these are what this world says make us significant. We needn't buy that lie.

Of course, Jesus calls us to so much more than monotonous conforming. We follow Him on the adventurous path of transforming. Take a look in the proverbial mirror: Do I look more like everyone else or more like Jesus?

> **LIFE IN A GODLESS WORLD IS UNORIGINAL, PREDICTABLE AND NOT WORTHY OF OUR CONFORMITY OR COMPLIANCE.**

---WE PRAY---

"Father, I am clay in Your hands, not poured into the mold of this world."

WHAT GOOD WILL IT BE FOR SOMEONE TO GAIN THE WHOLE WORLD, YET FORFEIT THEIR SOUL? OR WHAT CAN ANYONE GIVE IN EXCHANGE FOR THEIR SOUL?
[MATTHEW 16:26]

Our priorities are, by definition, exclusionary. That which we consider most important will displace in our thoughts and resources that which then becomes secondary. In other words, we're always making an exchange. We devote ourselves to our priorities to the natural neglect of other pursuits.

Spiritual matters aren't always seen as a priority. They become easily crowded out by the comforts and concerns of our day-to-day lives. We can find such days stringing together and soon we realize we've spent much of our lives making secondary things primary—to the neglect of our eternal souls. Consider today: How can I ensure I'm putting first things first and not exchanging the precious health of my soul for the lesser wealth of the world?

> **THIS WORLD MAY SEEM TO OFFER MUCH, BUT WHAT IT ULTIMATELY YIELDS US IS EMPTY AND WASTED LIVES.**

---WE PRAY---

"Lord, nothing is more precious to me than my soul's salvation in You."

> ...THE SPIRIT OF TRUTH. THE WORLD CANNOT ACCEPT HIM, BECAUSE IT NEITHER SEES HIM NOR KNOWS HIM. BUT YOU KNOW HIM, FOR HE LIVES WITH YOU AND WILL BE IN YOU.
> [JOHN 14:17]

A beautiful and amazing thing happens when we become followers of Jesus: His Spirit takes up residence in us, filling us and guiding us. This indwelling Spirit automatically sets us apart. We now walk to a rhythm those without His Spirit simply cannot yet hear. It's the soundtrack of our Rebellion.

Think of it as a radio frequency only we are tuned to receive. It's broadcast to all the world, but it's only through Jesus we can dial in. We have a new source of truth, a new and deeper way of understanding. Prayerfully ponder: How can I "tune in" more clearly to the Spirit's presence in me today?

> **WE SIMPLY LIVE IN AN ALTERNATE REALITY. BUT IT IS AN ACCURATE ONE, BASED ON THE TRUTH OF THE SPIRIT.**

---WE PRAY---

"Holy Spirit, in this world that's blind and confused, fill me with Your truth."

DO NOT LOVE THE WORLD OR ANYTHING IN THE WORLD. IF ANYONE LOVES THE WORLD, LOVE FOR THE FATHER IS NOT IN THEM.
[1 JOHN 2:15]

Our loving of people and things—what used to be called our "affections"—is a core determinant of our character. What stirs and inspires us, what draws and attracts us, is where we set our affections. And, not unlike in a marriage relationship, we're called to a fidelity in our love for God that precludes love for the world.

There are many things in this world to enjoy, but we should love nothing more than God. And whatever we truly, deeply love should be that which He has given, appreciated in the context of His grace. Ask yourself: Is there anything in my life vying for my affections and competing with my love for God?

> **OUR AFFECTIONS INEVITABLY FILL OUR HEARTS AND LEAD OUR LIVES. WHAT WE LOVE DIRECTS WHO WE BECOME.**

---WE PRAY---

"Father, may my love for You eclipse my affection for anything else."

> DON'T YOU KNOW THAT FRIENDSHIP WITH THE
> WORLD MEANS ENMITY AGAINST GOD?
> THEREFORE, ANYONE WHO CHOOSES TO BE A
> FRIEND OF THE WORLD BECOMES AN ENEMY OF GOD.
> [JAMES 4:4]

While we're not at war with culture or "the world" per se (this paradigm hasn't really served us very well), how friendly should we be with the world and its ways? Just how comfortable should we get with this culture so often antagonistic to God?

These are questions each disciple must answer on his or her own. However, the principle behind such inquiries is solid: we form our culture (the value system, worldview, and "language" we adopt) and then our culture forms us. This is true for us all. Reflect on it: Would Christ feel at home in the "culture" of my life? How at home am I in a prevailing culture that ignores or denies God?

> **WHEN WE GET TOO FAMILIAR OR COMFORTABLE WITH THIS WORLD, WE LOSE SIGHT OF WHOSE WE ARE AND WHY.**

---— WE PRAY ———

"God, keep me uncomfortable with this world and its ways."

For everything in the world— the lust of the flesh, the lust of the eyes, and the pride of life—comes not from the Father but from the world.
[1 John 2:16]

Biblically speaking, "the world" is any way of thinking and behaving that excludes the One True God and makes sin seem normal or acceptable. Apart from God, we are naturally disposed to consume and enjoy what this world offers. We need to consider what we're ingesting and check the label, so to speak. Is it coming from the Father or the world?

But we're not apart from God. He is near us, living *in* us. So we are thoughtful about what we let into our lives and careful about what we consume, considering its source. Give it some thought: In what am I partaking that's feeding my unhealthy appetites?

> **THIS WORLD'S SYSTEM OF SELFISHNESS, SENSUALITY, AND SUCCESS IS COMPLETELY COUNTER TO GOD'S GOODNESS.**

---WE PRAY---

"Father, let my heart be set on You and not be attracted to this world."

7
FOCUS ON FOREVER

I have tremendous admiration for Katie Davis and love her story. She traveled to Uganda on a mission trip when she was 18 years old, then moved there, then adopted 13 girls when she was 22 years old. She's married now, expanding her family, and still in Uganda running the large and thriving ministry she founded.

She's written honestly about her move, when she was still a teenager back in 2007. I'll quote her at length because she captures so well what I hope to convey in this chapter.

> You know what I want sometimes? To go to the mall and spend a ridiculous amount of money on a cute new pair of shoes. I want to sit on my kitchen counter chatting with my girlfriends and eat a whole carton of cookie dough ice cream. I want to hop in my cute car, go to the grocery store, and pick up any kind of produce I want. I want to... pick out a movie to watch with my little brother and his friends and I want to cook for them at midnight. I want my hair to look nice. I want to be a normal teenager living in America. I do.
>
> But. You know what I want more? ALL the time? I want to be spiritually and emotionally filled every day of my life. I want to be loved and cuddled by 100 children and never go a day without laughing. I want

to wake up to a rooster, my two African dogs, and a splendid view of the Nile River. I want to be challenged endlessly; I want to be learning and growing every minute. I want to share God's love with people who otherwise might not know it. I want to work so hard that I end every day filthy and too tired to move. I want to make a difference and I want to follow the calling that God has planted deep in my heart. I want to give my life away, to serve the Lord with each breath, each second. I want to be here. Right here.[1]

> IN OUR HUMANNESS, WE HAVE AN INSTINCT TO ASSIGN PERMANENCE TO THINGS OR CIRCUMSTANCES WHICH ARE IN FACT TERRIBLY TEMPORARY.

We're encountering a reality, a truth, each of us as keepers of the Way of Jesus need to get right. Katie Davis has gotten it right. Do we need to move to Uganda to get this right? Of course not. But there *is* a move we each need to make. As we follow Jesus and learn to make sense of life, this is a quandary we will face again and again until and unless we get a handle on it. When we don't, the consequences can be tough.

Let's redefine what wealth and success really are by taking the long view and seeing the big picture. If we are to keep to the Way, you and I absolutely must arrive at a point where we come to terms with how we are going to define success and fulfillment and handle wealth and possessions.

WE HAVE TO FINALLY FIGURE OUT WHAT'S TEMPORARY AND WHAT'S PERMANENT.

It's so easy for any of us to look around at what currently is or what we currently have and begin to feel as if it will last—maybe not forever, but—for as long as we want or need it to. We subtly tell ourselves that what is will always be. We wouldn't say it, but we can behave often as if it's true, living our days and setting our priorities as if it's true. In our humanness, we have an instinct to assign permanence to things or circumstances which are in fact terribly temporary. We do this mostly because we can't bear to face the truth of their impermanence. It's a natural, though not helpful, tendency we all share at some level. There is much to be enjoyed in our earthly life, much to thank God for and receive as good gifts from His hand (see James 1:17). But proper perspective is needed and must be consciously chosen, as Paul coached Timothy regarding pastoring his flock:

> Command those who are rich in this present world not to be arrogant nor to put their hope in wealth, which is so uncertain, but to put their hope in God, who richly provides us with everything for our enjoyment. (1 Timothy 6:17)

The snare of worldly wealth is its seeming promise of security, one of our most basic human needs. It's no wonder we're tempted to put our hope there. "The security we crave would teach us to rest our hearts in this world," C.S. Lewis observed. But we mustn't be driven by such cravings. "Our Father refreshes us on the journey with some pleasant inns, but will not encourage us to mistake them for home."[2] Until we comprehend this truth, we will keep investing ourselves in disappointments.

We must be relentlessly reminded: "This world in its present form is passing away." (1 Corinthians 7:31) Though not everything is passing away, to be sure. God and God's Word endure. His Kingdom has no end. People are permanent. (Not, of course, our bodies, but people are so much more than that.) We ourselves are eternal souls. These are not of this world. These are not passing away. These are true wealth. And we can invest ourselves in such real, lasting treasure.

> **THE SNARE OF WORLDLY WEALTH IS ITS SEEMING PROMISE OF SECURITY, A BASIC HUMAN NEED. IT'S NO WONDER WE'RE TEMPTED TO PUT OUR HOPE THERE.**

Or we can (and certainly far too often do), as Jesus put it, "store up treasure on earth." And how does He describe treasure placed here? "Where moth and rust destroy, and where thieves break in a steal." (Matthew 6:19) In other words, reliably perishable. The alternative? "Store up for yourselves treasures in heaven," where such destruction and theft are impossible. (Matthew 6:20) The apostle John essentially restates this investment choice in his first epistle: "The world and its desires pass away, but whoever does the will of God lives forever." (1 John 2:17)

Here we see described the difference between what's temporary and what's permanent. The world is a place of fleeting and fickle "desires," but there is a firm and steady path, that narrow Way Jesus calls us to. It is an eternal, life-giving Way. On it, people take solid action and do the will of God. Pursuing and doing God's will is how we store heavenly treasures, and how we keep the Way. "For where your treasure is," Jesus concluded, "there your heart will be also." (Matthew 6:21)

When we finally figure out what's permanent, it becomes clear what's worth giving our lives. And, of course, to "give your life" is really to give your days, each and any day of our lives. We can't let such phrases slip into the abstract. The way I live my life today reflects what I am indeed giving my life to. This is not a theory or slogan or generalized concept: "I give my life to this or that," or even "I gave my life to Jesus." What I devote my days to is what I give my life to in the most real of ways.

> **WE MUST KEEP BRINGING OURSELVES BACK TO THE ETERNAL PERSPECTIVE OF THE ONE WHO WAS EARTH-BORN BUT REFUSED TO BE EARTH-BOUND.**

We must keep bringing ourselves back to the eternal perspective of Jesus—this One who was earth-born but refused to be earth-bound. That's who we need walking with us. Recall His words to Martha as she grieved her brother's death, "Whoever lives by believing in me will never die. Do you believe this?" (John 11:26) He offers His wider point-of-view and asks if she can receive it as true, truer than what she can see on her own. *There is a way that leads to death, but it's not the only way. There is another; it transcends the boundaries of this world and rebels against its consequences. Will you,* Jesus asks us, *join Me on it?*

Do we believe we will never really die? That we are not temporary but eternal? That our lives—starting today—go on forever? Living in light of eternity is not always easy, to say the least. That's why we are to continually refocus our thoughts through Scripture and prayer and gathering with fellow disciples. We need consistently reminded that there is much more to this world than what we spend our days and nights watching and listening to and striving for. We need to reconnect with the eternal. Keeping to the Way means keeping our eyes on Jesus, fixated on His endless future for us.

Our growing discernment regarding what goes in the *temporary* category and what should be considered *permanent* will provide a radical contrast to the myopia of this world and make us substantively different than those yet without Christ. It should affect our priorities and our practices. Too often this is not the case, as Tom Sine has observed:

> Whatever commands our time, energy, and resources commands us. And if we are honest, we will admit that our lives really aren't that different from those of our secular counterparts. …We are so much like the people around us that we have very little to which we can call them. We hang around church buildings a little more. We abstain from a few things. But we simply aren't that different.[3]

OUR DISCERNMENT REGARDING WHAT'S TEMPORARY AND WHAT'S PERMANENT SHOULD PROVIDE A RADICAL CONTRAST TO THIS WORLD'S MYOPIA.

This is certainly a word of conviction regarding how we spend "our energy, time, and resources," how—or rather, where—we store up treasure. I don't want to paint us all with the same broad brush, but at least we can all recognize that we have the potential to be what Sine is describing.

When we get this wrong, our spiritual growth is stunted, and our witness is too.

Christian Smith and Hilary Davidson, researchers at Notre Dame's Science of Generosity Initiative, wrote *The Paradox of Generosity (Giving We Receive, Grasping We Lose)*. It's a super-interesting book full of all the charts and graphs you'd expect. The authors document how limited generosity really is in our culture, how only a tiny fraction of the population truly generously gives away their resources for the greater good. But their key observation—which is very pertinent to our discussion here—goes much deeper than that.

> Generosity is paradoxical. *Those who give, receive back in turn.* By *spending ourselves* for others' well-being, we enhance our own standing. In *letting go* of some of what we own, we ourselves move toward flourishing. This is not only a philosophical or religious teaching; it is a sociological fact. (*emphasis* mine)

Anyone sincerely searching for truth and reality will inevitably find themselves bumping into the teaching of Jesus. He's always known what these researchers have discovered: "It is more blessed to give than to receive." (Acts 20:35) Their choice of words, "spending ourselves" and "letting go" resonate with Jesus' call to discipleship. Spiritual truths and sociological facts are easily correlated, really one and the same to the thoughtful observer.

It is good to be generous; it is helpful. We Christians already know this and believe we have a Father who knows best, a Creator who knows how human life is supposed to function and "move toward flourishing." When God instructs us in His Word to be generous, He does so because it's best for us and grows us as healthy people by any measure, sociological or otherwise. These authors' findings bear this out:

> **ANYONE SINCERELY SEARCHING FOR TRUTH AND REALITY WILL INEVITABLY FIND THEMSELVES BUMPING INTO JESUS.**

> [In] failing to care for others, we do not properly take care of ourselves. ...We find consistent evidence that ungenerous lifestyles associate with an apathy riddled by anxiety. ...It is no coincidence that the word "miser" is etymologically related to the word "miserable."[4]

"Apathy riddled by anxiety" is sadly a description of so many who do indeed suffer so much misery. This challenge doesn't go away when we become Christians; indeed, the stakes actually get higher. The world views resources in terms of scarcity, but we account things differently. Our Father is rich, and we can give without stopping because He does the same. Generosity is not only good for us, but good for the world. It is love expressed most tangibly, and a potent witness of our generous, abundant God.

Here we should return to one of Jesus' most potent parables. In it He describes the Word of God coming to human hearts as seed that's sown into a variety of soils. We can see ourselves in His description and ask ourselves: What kind of soil, what condition of heart, are we cultivating? Consider this particular description: "The seed that fell among thorns stands for those who hear, but as they go on their way they are choked by life's worries, riches and pleasures, and they do not mature." (Luke 8:14)

This can be any of us as we hear the good word and *go on our way* (perhaps a telling phrase). We become "choked..and do not mature." That should get our attention. His diagnosis is precise and penetratingly accurate. We all have *worries*; most of us have (or desire) *riches*; we almost instinctively gravitate toward *pleasures* wherever they are promised.

> **MOST OF THE TIME, THE STUFF WE OWN ENDS UP OWNING US.**

If we have never really cleared out these distractions from our hearts, we are like a seedbed choked by thornbushes. God's Word is designed to grow in us, to change us and mature us so we can thrive. And yet it is imminently possible—and probable without concerted attention and effort on our part— that we'll remain stunted in our growth and immature in our faith (or even regress in that direction) if we don't break the chokehold of our possessions and become generous people.

WE LET GO OF EARTHLY ATTACHMENTS AND PURSUITS, WHICH NEVER LAST.

As we begin to get a handle on this truth, we learn what to hang on to and what to let go of. This unfolding realization touches our relationships, our ambitions, and , yes, our possessions. Most of the time, the stuff we own ends up owning us, owning our thoughts, time, and attention, owning our resources and even our affection.

Paul put it starkly: "For we brought nothing into the world, and we can take nothing out of it." (1 Timothy 6:7) Since our possessions no longer posses us, something else can, or rather Someone else does. And we begin to understand that no matter what we have or don't have, if we have God we have enough, indeed more than enough. As A.W. Tozer has so poignantly written, this is what Jesus was describing when he observed: "Blessed are the poor in spirit: for theirs is the kingdom of heaven." (Matthew 5:3)

> The blessed ones who possess the Kingdom are they who have repudiated every external thing and have rooted from their hearts all sense of possessing. These are the "poor in spirit." ...These blessed poor are no longer slaves to the tyranny of things... "Theirs is the kingdom of heaven."

Tozer reinforces our premise in terms keeping with the imagery of this book. This renunciation of the earthly in order to focus on the eternal is not a practice reserved for only the most spiritually devout, but for every keeper of the Way.

> Let me exhort you to take this seriously. ...It is a marker on the road to greener pastures, a path chiseled against the steep sides of the mount of God. We dare not try to bypass it if we would follow on the holy pursuit. We must ascend a step at a time. If we refuse one step, we bring progress to an end.[5]

Again, Jesus' captures the dynamic perfectly: "For the pagan world runs after all such things, and your Father knows that you need them." (Luke 12:30) There is a broad way, really a treadmill, on which this world "runs after all such things." We are surrounded by the empty pursuits of a society that negates or ignores God. Always running and never arriving, it's a non-stop culture of consuming, purchasing, acquiring. It is easy to chase stuff, but stuff ultimately doesn't matter and certainly cannot satisfy. Only One can...and will. We have a Provider, and it's not all up to us. This is the foundation of not only trusting peace, but true generosity. Fully internalizing the truth that our Father knows

> **RENOUNCING THE EARTHLY IN ORDER TO FOCUS ON THE ETERNAL IS NOT RESERVED FOR ONLY THE MOST DEVOUT.**

what we need will keep us from distractedly darting here, there, and everywhere, pursuing possessions and leaving the Way.

C.S. Lewis offered an interesting slant on how we get tangled in the consumerism trap. In *The Screwtape Letters*, the demon Screwtape has the job of mentoring his protégé Wormwood in their ways of seducing humans to their eternal doom. He counsels Wormwood that by playing on their addiction to the pursuit of "prosperity," humans can be brought to their destruction.

> Prosperity knits a man to the World. He feels that he is "finding his place in it," while really it is finding its place in him. His increasing reputation, his widening circle of acquaintances, his sense of importance, the growing pressure of absorbing and agreeable work, build up in him a sense of being really at home on earth, which is just what we want.[6]

Lewis warns us that our concern with popularity and prosperity can cause us to become entangled with the world, hanging onto the very things of which we should be letting go. Such entanglement crowds out the presence of the Holy Spirit in us. We can begin to feel that our esteem is measured by the opinions of others and that our self worth is tied to our net worth. If we're not vigilant, prosperity can dull our resistance and dim our rebellious spirit. It lulls us into believing this world is our home. It is not.

> **IF WE'RE NOT VIGILANT, PROSPERITY CAN DULL OUR RESISTANCE AND DIM OUR REBELLIOUS SPIRIT.**

WE ARE FREE TO DEDICATE OURSELVES TO REAL WORK AND LASTING IMPACT.

This is the best part. The Rebellion isn't merely about bucking the status quo of consumerism. Self-denial and non-conformity are a means, never an end. It's empty religion that creates rules for no reason. What we're talking about is so much more. It's about making room in our hearts for what really matters. When I'm entangled, distracted, and "choked by life's worries, riches, and pleasures," I'm drained of the energy required make a real difference in the world. God wants us to get these things out of our way because He has some serious work for us to do.

You see, selfishness shrinks us. Sin reduces us. Society compresses us into its confining mold. We might think that by this world's standards we're big stuff or that we've hit the big time, but when we do, our universe is constricted and our impact is neutralized. This does no one, including ourselves, any good.

The Resistance isn't repressive, it's freeing. Life in Christ is expansive, radiating outward, glowing. And the Rebellion isn't about retreating from the world but engaging with it. Though the Way of Christ is non-conforming, it is also compelling.

Earlier we read Tom Sine rightly lament that far too often how we Christians spend our time, energy, and resources differs very little from those without the blessing of Christ's wisdom or the responsibility of His mission. He goes on:

> As a result of this unfortunate accommodation, Christianity is reduced to little more than a spiritual crutch. ...God is there to help us get our promotions, our house in the suburbs, and our bills paid. Somehow God has become a co-conspirator in our agendas instead of our becoming a co-conspirator in His. Something is seriously amiss.[7]

We can easily slip into seeing God as the One who helps us achieve our goals instead of pledging ourselves to achieving His. This is the way much of the world thinks of God—or at least the idea of God—if He's thought of at all. Our Rebellion includes rejecting this "unfortunate accommodation" and reduction of our vibrant Christian faith.

> **SELFISHNESS SHRINKS US. SIN REDUCES US. SOCIETY COMPRESSES US INTO ITS CONFINING MOLD.**

We're the ones who realize there's a Revolution quietly running rampant, a movement—God doing what God does—in hearts and societies and nations, and ask ourselves: How can I join Him in that? I want to be part of His plan, not just ask Him to endorse mine. I cover this more fully in the next and final section, but here is where it starts.

The fact is, we can be thoughtless. One Sunday at our church, our missionaries in Venezuela were with us. Jorge shared stories of danger and risk and scarcity: a truck riddled with bullet holes, the lack of basic household necessities, bars on bedroom windows. No sooner than immediately after that service dismissed I heard from one of our café servers that someone was complaining about our doughnut selection. There are countless ways we can miss the point, and some days we may do so countless times. Thank God for His empowering grace that enables us to try again to get it right and push against this downward pull and inward collapsing.

Recall the poignant way Paul described to the Philippians the foes of our faith: "Their destiny is destruction, their god is their stomach, and their glory is in their shame. Their mind is set on earthly things." The destined destruction Paul foretells here is the same destination to which the broad road leads, according to Jesus. It's the lot of those who "run after all such things." Paul says such people worship their

> **THERE ARE COUNTLESS WAYS WE CAN MISS THE POINT, AND SOME DAYS WE MAY DO SO COUNTLESS TIMES. THANK GOD FOR HIS EMPOWERING GRACE.**

appetites and celebrate whatever satiates them, however base. Their stomach, not their heart, is their center. And their feet are nailed to the floor, their mind bound to earth. Paul makes the contrast clear:

> But our citizenship is in heaven. And we eagerly await a Savior from there, the Lord Jesus Christ, who, by the power that enables him to bring everything under his control, will transform our lowly bodies so that they will be like his glorious body. (Philippians 3:18-21)

It is this transformation from the temporary to the eternal that we will not only experience on that great Day, but we can begin to experience in countless ways today and every day.

We are built to make an impact, made for mission. When we let go of stuff, our hands can be open to put to the plow (see Luke 9:62). When we fix our eyes on the prize (see 1 Corinthians 9:24 and Philippians 3:14), we're no longer duped by this world's empty definitions of success, wealth, and fulfillment. Our hearts can be ready to move forward and do the work of God.

This orientation toward the long view and the big picture is key to navigating life on the Way. We continually ask ourselves: Temporary or eternal? What matters, what doesn't matter? What's worthy of my life's investment, what isn't? Who am I, and who am I becoming?

There's a great moment between Jesus and His disciples in John chapter four. It's one of my favorite things Jesus says. The crew is back from getting lunch. He's been having a deeply spiritual conversation with a woman at a well. They offer Him a bite to eat and He's not interested. They wonder: Has He already eaten? Did someone bring Him food? But Jesus is satisfied in deeper ways and shares His perspective with them: "My food is to do the will of him who sent me and to finish his work." (John 4:34) That's where I find my fulfillment, He says. Indeed, Jesus redefines fulfillment for us all.

Remember, it's not that we have to pretend we don't want stuff or enjoy certain things. Like Katie Davis admitted, there are plenty of things that look pretty good or sound pretty fun to us. And there's nothing wrong with them. It's just that, like Katie, we can discover we want something else more, realize there is something more worthy of our energy and more fulfilling to our soul. There's much to enjoy in the here and now, and much work to do. We savor what's truly good and we labor in our Father's fields, all the time with one eye on eternity, focused on forever.

THIS WORLD IN ITS PRESENT FORM IS PASSING AWAY.
[1 CORINTHIANS 7:31]

It's easy to get caught up in what's fashionable and popular, whether it be the latest looks or gadgets, or more substantive matters like philosophies and ethics. However, as followers of Jesus we are consistently reminded by Scripture: everything that's trending will soon be ending.

Our lives are an investment. This Rebellion means not following the market and squandering our resources on a bubble that will inevitably burst. We take the long view. We've discovered what's secure and lasts forever, so we deposit ourselves there. Take an inventory: In what ways might I be placing far too much stock in that which will one day cease to exist and matter not at all?

> **WHEN WE GET TOO CAUGHT UP IN THIS WORLD'S PRIORITIES AND PURSUITS, WE FORGET WHAT TRULY LASTS FOREVER.**

---WE PRAY---

"Jesus, help me build my life on Your solid, lasting truth."

THE WORLD AND ITS DESIRES PASS AWAY, BUT WHOEVER DOES THE WILL OF GOD LIVES FOREVER.
[1 JOHN 2:17]

To follow Jesus is to live in alignment with God's will, to tap into the eternal, to resonate with the deepest purposes and pleasures possible. By contrast, to follow the world is to endlessly search for what's meaningful and to chase our impulsive cravings to their disappointing ends.

Disciples delight to simply and humbly do God's will. It is so good and healthy and wise. And, lest we forget, it brings life that never stops. Remember Jesus' words to Martha: "Whoever lives by believing in me will never die." (John 11:26) Ask yourself: Which of my dreams and ambitions will come to nothing in light of the fact that I get to live forever?

> **SO MANY DESIRES AND FANTASIES DISTRACT US, BUT THE BEAUTY OF GOD'S TRUTH IS ETERNALLY CAPTIVATING.**

---WE PRAY---

"God, my appetites and aspirations are fickle, but Your will is perfectly good."

> THE SEED THAT FELL AMONG THORNS STANDS FOR
> THOSE WHO HEAR, BUT AS THEY GO ON THEIR WAY
> THEY ARE CHOKED BY LIFE'S WORRIES, RICHES
> AND PLEASURES, AND THEY DO NOT MATURE.
> [LUKE 8:14]

Many hear God's Word and even answer Christ's call to follow Him, but they do not partner with God to cultivate a life that will actually flourish in His Way. Their hearts have been seeded but not weeded. So the "worries, riches, and pleasures" of this world leave little ground for God's truth to take root and bear fruit. Their growth is stunted. Jesus' parable makes it clear: this is not who any of us want to be.

We rightly rebel when we choose to no longer be distracted by such things and refuse to allow them to choke God's life out of us. Consider: What exactly is holding me back from serious spiritual growth?

> **GOD'S WORD FLOURISHES IN OUR HEARTS TO THE EXTENT WE REMOVE DISTRACTIONS AND GIVE IT ROOM TO GROW.**

---WE PRAY---

"Lord, let my growth not be stunted by the secondary and temporary."

FOR WE BROUGHT NOTHING INTO THE WORLD, AND WE CAN TAKE NOTHING OUT OF IT.
[1 TIMOTHY 6:7]

The lure of worldly wealth can be strong. Any of us can start to believe the empty promise that life's meaning and success are found in accumulating cool stuff and creature comforts. But earthly life is brief, and after it we stand before our Creator bare and without a thread of our material wardrobe.

The best we can do is convert the temporal and physical into the eternal and spiritual. We can use our wealth—whatever its size—to fuel the cause of Christ. Generous giving is a potent way of breaking the allure riches can have on us. Check your balance: Am I living as though my net worth will be worth anything at all in the end?

> **IT'S EASY TO BE POSSESSED BY OUR POSSESSIONS, BUT IN CHRIST THE WORDS "MY" AND "MINE" LOSE THEIR MEANING.**

---WE PRAY---

"Lord, I won't be fooled by prosperity or discouraged by poverty."

> FOR THE PAGAN WORLD RUNS
> AFTER ALL SUCH THINGS, AND YOUR
> FATHER KNOWS THAT YOU NEED THEM.
> [LUKE 12:30]

So if our Rebellion includes our refusal to be baited by the materialism this world chases, then such refusal must be grounded in deep trust of our Father God. This is how we escape the "rat race" so many run: we know God knows what we need.

While we should be diligent workers and wise stewards, providing for ourselves is not all up to us. We have a Provider. We pursue Him and His will; we don't run after things. That's the direction in which this whole world is careening. We know better because we know Him. Contemplate this: What and whom am I running after? In what ways am I chasing when I should be trusting?

> **OUR TRUST IN GOD FREES US FROM THIS WORLD'S OBSESSION WITH STUFF AND TEMPORARY SATISFACTION.**

---WE PRAY---

"Father, may my pursuits please You and testify to my trust in You."

> BUT OUR CITIZENSHIP IS IN HEAVEN.
> AND WE EAGERLY AWAIT A SAVIOR FROM THERE...
> [PHILIPPIANS 3:20]

It's not that our actions and their consequences in this world don't matter, indeed they matter tremendously. When we go against the flow, we create a ripple effect that can make a true difference not only in our lives but in many others' lives. However, as followers of Jesus, we're not *from* here anymore. We are, as He said to Nicodemus, "born from above." (John 3:3)

This world is not our home, but neither are we "merely passing through." We're occupying territory—prayerfully more and more of it—until our Commander returns. Assess yourself: Do I see myself as a citizen and regent of my Father's Kingdom on assignment in a foreign land?

> **THIS WORLD IS NOW TO US FOREIGN SOIL. WE LIVE HERE AS AMBASSADORS OF THE ONE TRUE AND COMING KING.**

---WE PRAY---

"I look to You, my Savior and my Sovereign, and pledge my allegiance to You."

8
BELONG TOGETHER

According to the most recent stats from US State Department, Christians in more than 60 countries face persecution from their governments or surrounding neighbors simply because of their belief in Jesus Christ. In some of these nations it is illegal to own a Bible, to share your faith Christ, or teach your children about Jesus. Those who boldly follow Christ—in spite of government edict or radical opposition—can face harassment, arrest, torture, and even death.[1]

In some parts of the world today this persecution is severe. Christians are being brutalized, abused, and even crucified. The details of these offences are extremely disturbing to say the least. But it is happening right now. The stories we hear and read of unbelievable strength and faith in the face of the ultimate test of devotion are equal parts inspiring and infuriating. Martyrs for Christ who pray and sing aloud and lift their heads and proclaim the name "Jesus!" as they are raped, abused, and slaughtered because they refuse to renounce Him. They are in every deepest sense keepers of the Way.

When confronted with such brutal facts we ask: What can we do? We can pray. We cannot be silent. We can and must remember our suffering brothers and sisters around the world. We don't face what they face, at least not yet—and we don't know, maybe not ever in our lifetimes. But nevertheless, we too can keep to the Way and go against the flow, whatever that looks like in our world, in our lives today.

Together we face the opposition and rejection of this world. We know it's not where we belong. It's time to put on our big kid pants and stop complaining about inconveniences or things not going according to our preferences and be Christians, strong and mature, clear-headed and clean-hearted.

THE GOSPEL OF JESUS IS OFFENSIVE TO HUMAN PRIDE AND SELF-SUFFICIENCY.

This truth is foundational to our discussion here. The message of Jesus is repugnant to the human ego. It always has been. To receive forgiveness, we must at least admit we need it. Such an admission of being not only guilty but (considered even worse) misguided and incorrect runs counter to the humanistic hubris that inflates so many today. (We can be like the Fonz on *Happy Days*, physically unable to say the words, "I'm wrong" or "I'm sorry."[2])

Jesus assessed our situation and described it to Nicodemus like this: "This is the verdict: Light has come into the world, but people loved darkness instead of light because their deeds were evil." (John 3:19) This describes any of us before we turned to Jesus, all of humanity without Jesus. But in Christ, everything is illuminated. Yet our first instinct as humans is to hide from a holy God, like Adam and Even in the garden after they went their own way. However, the invitation God initiates is always to step into the light and then to be bearers of that light. Healthy things grow in such light; unhealthy things in us shrivel and die in that same light.

> **THE MESSAGE OF JESUS HAS ALWAYS BEEN REPUGNANT TO THE HUMAN EGO. TO RECEIVE FORGIVENESS WE MUST AT LEAST ADMIT WE NEED IT.**

It's when we decide to keep alive and growing in us that which we'd be better off losing, when we choose to harbor some sin and selfishness, that we "love darkness instead of light." And our opportunity to bear such light—not self-righteously, but sincerely—is missed. But when we are illuminated, when—almost literally—the light comes on for us in our heads, our hearts, our souls, we can joyfully and convincingly invite others to step into the light too.

It's in the shadowlands at the borders of light and darkness that conflict and tension rises. Many love darkness, and thus feel hatred for the luminous.

Jesus referred to this when he said, "If the world hates you, keep in mind that it hated me first." (John 15:18) *Hate* sounds pretty rough, but it is a reality. It was painfully real to Jesus, just as real to the first Christians, and equally real today. Remember Paul's words to the Philippians: "For, as I have often told you before and now tell you again even with tears, many live as enemies of the cross of Christ." (Philippians 3:18) This is as true today as it ever has been.

As Proverbs 14:9 states bluntly, "Fools mock at making amends for sin."

> **WHO WE ARE HAS VERY MUCH TO DO WITH WHOSE WE ARE.**

Human pride will always rise up and make fun of the belief that we don't know best and that what we want most may be worst for us. Even more irritating to our misplaced dignity is the idea that we owe something for our shortcomings.

A godless society will always find the Gospel offensive. Remember: the world wanted to silence Jesus when He was here in the flesh. The world still wants to silence Jesus as He is here in the Church. This is our harsh and heartbreaking reality.

We are a heavenly community of redeemed people, accepted by God and outcasts to the world.

Jesus tells us why we're hated: We don't belong here. "If you belonged to the world, it would love you as its own. As it is, you do not belong to the world, but I have chosen you out of the world. That is why the world hates you." (John 15:19) Who we are has very much to do with whose we are.

We all want to belong. Just recall Maslow's hierarchy of needs from Psy 101. And as Jesus says, the world will lavish its love, however fickle, on those who make themselves at home in it. But when keepers of the Way—by simply and humbly following Jesus on His slim path—essentially say to this world that we don't need it or need to belong in it, the response to such God-sufficiency is vehement. "You don't need all we have to offer?" we may hear in one form or another. "Who do you think you are? Are you better than we are?"

Of course, such a reaction stems from an insecurity that fears perhaps we Christians really have found something better. Indeed, we have. However, the important distinction we can live out before the world is that we didn't find this Way because we're better; we're better only because we found this Way. No one knows as well as we do how bad off we were without it. And how much we need our fellow followers as we keep to it.

In the original Greek the word *church* is *ecclesia*, meaning "the called out ones." This verb *chosen* we heard Jesus use in John 15:19 has the same root word as the noun *church*. Jesus has chosen to call us, the Church, "out of the world." We're not the chosen ones as in the preferred ones and as opposed to the rejected ones. We're the ones who've accepted the invitation, understood Jesus to say to each of us "I've chosen to call you out," knowing He says it to all who will listen. It is from that posture we live in this world too often deaf to such truth. We live to let them know: *He's calling you. He's chosen you, too.*

> **WE'RE BETTER ONLY BECAUSE WE FOUND THIS WAY. NO ONE KNOWS AS WELL AS WE DO HOW BAD OFF WE WERE WITHOUT IT.**

Peter paints a picture of the contrast created between the world and Jesus' called-out-ones. He admonishes in his first epistle:

> For you have spent enough time in the past doing what pagans choose to do—living in debauchery, lust, drunkenness, orgies, carousing and detestable idolatry. They are surprised that you do not join them in their reckless, wild living, and they heap abuse on you. But they will have to give account to him who is ready to judge the living and the dead. (1 Peter 4:3-5)

This world—on the whole—is going one way. And we as followers of Jesus are simply going another—no, more than that, *the other*—way, the opposite way. And we must remember that opposite can mean opposing and sometimes brings opposition.

We're rejecting the world's definitions of pleasure and success, rejecting the pursuit of fulfilling the appetites this world makes so primary. We're not out to reject people, but there's no softening the blow that we are indeed rejecting the prevailing worldview. And they "heap abuse" on us, mocking our convictions and portraying us as either ignorant or "holier-than-thou" and self-righteous when in all humility we are simply aiming to live a healthy life before God and make good choices, one day at a time, one day after another, one foot in front of the other, walking the Way.

However, these opposing forces mustn't be ignored or denied. As Dutch theologian and statesman Abraham Kuyper once said:

> When principles that run against your deepest convictions begin to win the day, then battle is your calling, and peace has become sin; you must, at the price of dearest peace, lay your convictions bare before friend and enemy, with all the fire of your faith.[3]

We're not at war with the culture, but our rebellion is not unlike a battle as we keep to the Way. Especially when, as Kuyper puts it, erroneous and unhealthy principles begin to become the common sense. Rebellion is the only sane and right response. That's at least one reason Paul called it fighting "the good fight of the faith" (1 Timothy 6:12) and exhorts us to "Be on your guard; stand firm in the faith; be courageous; be strong." (1 Corinthians 16:13) And Jesus did not say without reason, "Do not suppose that I have come to bring peace to the earth. I did not come to bring peace, but a sword." (Matthew 10:34)

As American Christians we've grown accustomed to a measure of peace, a self-assured—if sometimes self-deceived—feeling that our society basically agrees with us, that somehow going with the flow of our culture was mostly resonant with following Jesus and His Way. This may have at times in the past been more or less the case. Those days—if they ever existed at all—are over.

> **WHEN ERRONEOUS AND UNHEALTHY PRINCIPLES BECOME THE COMMON SENSE, REBELLION IS THE ONLY SANE RESPONSE.**

Just as the earliest Christians were pressured to be "good Romans" or face the consequences, so we feel from every side in a chorus of voices both loud and subtle the pressure to be a "good American" when what that means isn't what it used to mean, in many ways becoming a concept now barely recognizable. We must come to grips with this.

We must prepare ourselves to live in a society in which being a Jesus-follower is going to cost us, exact something from us, come at a price. A little later in Peter's letter we read:

> If you are insulted because of the name of Christ, you are blessed, for the Spirit of glory and of God rests on you. If you suffer, it should not be as a murderer or thief or any other kind of criminal, or even as a meddler. However, if you suffer as a Christian, do not be ashamed, but praise God that you bear that name. (1 Peter 4:14-16)

Most of us don't "suffer as a Christian," certainly not as the original readers of Peter's words did (though many around the world do). Criticism, perhaps, but not crucifixion. Mockery, but definitely not murder. However, whatever we suffer, if it's endured in the name of and because we walk in the Way of Jesus Christ, we are on a most blessed path, and we praise God that we bear that name. His Name. No one can take it away from us. It is ours for eternity.

> **THE REAL FUN BEGINS WHEN WE FINALLY REALIZE FITTING IN IS OVERRATED AND BORING.**

We get to bear the Name, shine the light, keep to the Way. That's who the Church truly is: redeemed people accepted by God and rejected by the world.

Though rebellion means rejection and opposition, both bring their own blessing.

When we go against the flow, we escape the pull of other people's opinions. They simply don't weigh what they used to, don't weigh on us as they once did. The goal is not to try to be abnormal or rebellious for their own sake. The goal is to follow Jesus, which will at times guarantee we don't fit in. The real fun begins when we finally realize that fitting in is overrated and boring, and that when we try to fit in, we give up so much more than we gain. This realization is a hugely pivotal aspect of the freedom Christ brings.

"Blessed are you when people insult you, persecute you and falsely say all kinds of evil against you because of me," Jesus taught. "Rejoice and be glad, because great is your reward in heaven, for in the same way they persecuted the prophets who were before you." (Matthew 5:11-12) These words are for all of His disciples, any of us following Jesus today. We realize that to just tell the truth, to just be an honest, transparent, sincere, and humble Jesus-follower, is in a very real sense to live in this world as a prophet. Prophets were and are truth-tellers. To be prophetic is to tell the truth no matter the cost. And there's almost always a cost.

Jesus also said, "Woe to you when all people speak well of you." (Luke 6:26) And as Paul told Timothy: "Everyone who wants to live a godly life in Christ Jesus will be persecuted." (2 Timothy 3:12) Persecution may not have yet reached us at its fullest force, but criticism or insults or slander...we can at least steel ourselves for more of these. What others think can become too important to us. It can drive us nuts if someone misunderstands us, gets the wrong idea about us. But eventually we learn we'll never control other people's opinions and can't live according to them. Our brothers and sisters around the globe suffer so much worse.

So we strive to be ourselves, that flourishing expression of all our wise and creative God designed us to be and leads us to do and become. And as much as we love people, we don't live our lives based on what they think. Maybe that's a lesson many learn with age, but the sooner we learn it, the better. Don't miss this essential lesson: If you live for the acceptance of others, you will find their rejection fatal. If we build our self-esteem on what others think of us, we feel demolished when someone thinks poorly of us. Yet such derision is exactly what Scripture warns us every disciple must endure. This reality pushes us toward the maturity which understands there must One whose opinion trumps all.

> **TO BE PROPHETIC IS TO TELL THE TRUTH NO MATTER THE COST. AND THERE'S ALMOST ALWAYS A COST.**

This One prepares us with words like these: "In this world you will have trouble. But take heart! I have overcome the world." (John 16:33) It's this never-wavering presence and support of Jesus that makes all the difference. Dietrich Bonhoeffer, who knew so much more than most about suffering persecution for his faith, wrote in *The Cost of Discipleship*:

The messengers of Jesus will be hated to the end of time. They will be blamed for all the division which rend cities and homes. Jesus and his disciples will be condemned on all sides for undermining family life, and for leading the nation astray; they will be called crazy fanatics and disturbers of the peace. The disciples will be sorely tempted to desert their Lord. But the end is also near, and they must hold on and persevere until it comes. Only he will be blessed who remains loyal to Jesus and his word until the end.[4]

Telling words for our time. Jesus said as much: "You will be hated by everyone because of me." When the pressure rises, we're tempted to hang back and ease up, to go with the flow. "But," He assures us, "the one who stands firm to the end will be saved." (Matthew 10:22)

Where does all this lead us? What does it all mean? It means we need each other. It leads us to conclude we can't go it alone.

WE ARE GALVANIZED BY SUCH PRESSURES AND WE HELP EACH OTHER KEEP THE FAITH.

It is essential we understand this if we are going to become and remain keepers of the Way. In all our talk about rebelling against the ways of this world and staying on the Way of Jesus, we begin to see clearly that the stakes of this journey we're on together are neither low nor inconsequential. Leaving the Way of Jesus is a serious thing, so we need to lovingly and honestly help each other stay on it. It's the only way we are changed and made whole; it's the only way the world gets changed and made healthy.

> **LEAVING THE WAY OF JESUS IS A SERIOUS THING, SO WE NEED TO LOVINGLY AND HONESTLY HELP EACH OTHER STAY ON IT.**

In a passage that perhaps isn't preached too often but is imminently insightful, we read these practical instructions:

> When I wrote to you before, I told you not to associate with people who indulge in sexual sin. But I wasn't talking about unbelievers who

indulge in sexual sin, or are greedy, or cheat people, or worship idols. You would have to leave this world to avoid people like that. (1 Corinthians 5:9-10 NLT)

We don't expect—and it's foolish and fruitless to even think about expecting—people who don't know Jesus to behave as though they do, to pass laws as though they do, to make decisions as though they do. They don't, just as you and I once did not. We were without Jesus and out-of-line in our thinking and behaving. Much of the world still is.

Paul is looking to rightsize our expectations of others and guide us regarding how to relate to them. We

> **IT'S FOOLISH AND FRUITLESS TO EXPECT PEOPLE WHO DON'T KNOW JESUS TO MAKE DECISIONS AS THOUGH THEY DO.**

aren't to avoid or reject people who aren't yet Christians, far from it. We are to embrace those Jesus embraced and invite them into His life. Paul's directive is speaking to something different. He's referring to people who call themselves Christians but choose not to keep to the Way.

> I meant that you are not to associate with anyone who claims to be a believer yet indulges in sexual sin, or is greedy, or worships idols, or is abusive, or is a drunkard, or cheats people. Don't even eat with such people. (1 Corinthians 5:11 NLT)

It's not because we love them less, quite the contrary. It's exactly because we love them that we remain straightforward with them. We may be the only ones left telling them the truth about their condition. In *The Message* paraphrase, Eugene Peterson captures very well what I believe Paul is saying here:

> I *am* saying that you shouldn't act as if everything is just fine when a friend who claims to be a Christian is promiscuous or crooked, is flip with God or rude to friends, gets drunk or becomes greedy and predatory. You can't just go along with this, treating it as acceptable behavior.

How do we as Christians live together in our Father's house? Paul is instructing us regarding the tough love we sometimes must show. We help each other stay on the Way in the most caring and forthright ways we can. It's part of what makes us a family: You don't simply stand by and let me screw up my life, and I don't let you either.

This doesn't mean putting others on an examination table, poking at and magnifying every little flaw we may find. But it does mean meeting each other at the communion table, calling each other to a healthy, God-honoring way of life, sharpening and inspiring each other, and transparently loving each other.

To quote Bonhoeffer one more time, this time from his book *Life Together*: "Nothing can be more cruel than the leniency which abandons others to their sin. Nothing can be more compassionate than the severe reprimand which calls another Christian in one's community back from the path of sin."[5] Can we accept that truth? We must. We must not let human pride, which keeps so much of the world rejecting the Gospel, rise up in us and keep us from staying with the Gospel. I believe we can discover deep unity and trust and love in such care for one another.

> **YOU AND I CAN'T STAND STRONG AND GO AGAINST THE FLOW OF THIS WORLD ON OUR OWN. IT'S SIMPLY NOT GOING TO HAPPEN.**

Friend, this is why a church family is so important. We belong together. We need each other. You and I aren't going to stand strong and go against the flow of this world on our own. It's simply not going to happen. We cannot go it alone, and we don't have to.

Worshiping, learning, and doing life together with fellow Christians must become a steady habit for us if we desire to keep to the Way. If we will develop it, we will find it to be a powerful habit, a keystone habit (to borrow a term I recently learned from Charles Duhigg in his book, *The Power of Habit*).

> Keystone habits start a process that, over time, transforms everything. [It] relies on identifying a few key priorities and fashioning them into powerful levers. ...The habits that matter most are the ones that, when they start to shift, dislodge and remake other patterns.[6]

"A process that, over time, transforms everything..." that's what we're aiming for. Disciplines that "dislodge and remake other patterns" make us a force for change. As the writer of Hebrews exhorted:

> Let us consider how we may spur one another on toward love and good deeds, not giving up meeting together, as some are in the habit of doing, but encouraging one another—and all the more as you see the Day approaching. (Hebrews 10:24-25)

I have found again and again, in myself and others, when we consistently make the decision to come to church, to connect with other believers, to form accountable and constructive relationships—to simply *be together*—it's like pressing the reset button of our souls. The long term effect is healthier, wiser lives as well as deeper, wider impact. One of the most "powerful levers" of our Rebellion is our unity.

There's so much we've considered in this chapter. Here's my hope and prayer for us all, our brutalized brothers and sisters around the world as well as you and me in our daily challenges and trials: "Stand firm in the one Spirit, striving together as one for the faith of the gospel without being frightened in any way by those who oppose you." (Philippians 1:27-28)

This is the path we're on. It's one of opposition because it runs opposite to the ways of this world. But it's also a path on which we can thrive and to which we can invite others. It's the way of rescue and wisdom we follow in Jesus. And we follow it *together*.

IF THE WORLD HATES YOU, KEEP IN MIND THAT IT HATED ME FIRST.
[JOHN 15:18]

People hated Jesus. Think about that. He was the embodiment of love, full of grace and truth, yet some people hated not only Him but His followers. This is no less true today. From where does this hatred come?

Some hate is borne of pain. Life can be very difficult and people blame God. At other times it comes from pride. People don't want to hear that they need God. And sometimes it's selfishness that wants to clutch the pleasure of sin and reject anyone who attempts to show a better way.

Such hatred is tragic and ugly and inevitable. And we students are not above our Teacher. Pause and reflect: How will I respond when my love for Jesus brings out hate in others?

> **WHEN OUR LOVE OF GOD RAISES THE IRE OF OUR CONTEMPORARIES, WE ARE IN THE BEST OF COMPANY.**

---WE PRAY---

"God, give me courage to stand for You and be counted as Yours."

AS I HAVE OFTEN TOLD YOU BEFORE AND NOW TELL YOU AGAIN EVEN WITH TEARS, MANY LIVE AS ENEMIES OF THE CROSS OF CHRIST.
[PHILIPPIANS 3:18]

In the passage quoted above, Paul says these enemies of Christ's cross worship their appetites and glory in their shameful acts. The cross is offensive to them because it calls for repentance, a heartfelt sorrow and turning from such living. As Proverbs 14:9 states bluntly, "Fools mock at making amends for sin." This is heartbreaking.

Disciples are people absolutely marked by the cross of Jesus. It is the hinge upon which our histories turn. We've learned the beauty of repentance and the deep meaning of Jesus' sacrificial death. Consider: When was the last time I wept because of others' antipathy toward the Gospel?

> **IT'S A GRIEVOUS REALITY THAT SO MANY NOT ONLY REJECT BUT RIDICULE THE PRECIOUS SACRIFICE OF OUR JESUS.**

WE PRAY

"Christ, I will humbly but boldly defend the beauty of what You did at Calvary."

> BLESSED ARE YOU WHEN PEOPLE INSULT YOU,
> PERSECUTE YOU AND FALSELY SAY ALL KINDS OF EVIL
> AGAINST YOU BECAUSE OF ME. REJOICE AND BE GLAD,
> BECAUSE GREAT IS YOUR REWARD IN HEAVEN,
> FOR IN THE SAME WAY THEY PERSECUTED
> THE PROPHETS WHO WERE BEFORE YOU.
> [MATTHEW 5:11-12]

Our Rebellion against the order of this world will not be achieved without injury and trauma. Jesus warns us to expect it. And more than that, He says we should be happy when it happens. Why? Because it means we're standing with Him and not giving in. Like any prophet of God and preacher of truth, we face contention. We can lean into the pain with a smile; He's been there and is in our corner.

To be counted as Christ's is its own reward. Scars earned in His service are badges of honor. Ask yourself: Am I ready to take a pay cut, take a punch, or take a bullet for my faith in Jesus?

PERSECUTION IS A SPECIAL PRIVILEGE IF IT MEANS BEING COUNTED AS A FAITHFUL FOLLOWER OF JESUS.

---WE PRAY---

"Jesus, I will rejoice when I face rejection because of my faith in You."

> IF YOU BELONGED TO THE WORLD,
> IT WOULD LOVE YOU AS ITS OWN.
> AS IT IS, YOU DO NOT BELONG TO THE WORLD,
> BUT I HAVE CHOSEN YOU OUT OF THE WORLD.
> [JOHN 15:19]

We have an innate need to belong. We will do almost anything to achieve it, to be appreciated or at least accepted. But apart from Christ that never ends well. The love of the world is fickle, and gaining it is a hollow accomplishment we no longer need pursue. Jesus gives us a new family to which we can belong. It's the best.

This family is the Church. It is our laboratory where we learn true love. It is our sanctuary where we find serenity amidst this tumultuous society.

We break this world's rules of engagement when we decide we no longer need its acceptance. Look within and ask: How strongly do I still hunger for this world's validation?

> **THE CHURCH IS THOSE WHO'VE ANSWERED CHRIST'S CALL TO LEAVE THE WORLD BEHIND. THIS IS WHERE WE BELONG.**

---WE PRAY---

"Jesus, thank You for choosing to open an exit out of this world."

> STAND FIRM IN THE ONE SPIRIT,
> STRIVING TOGETHER AS ONE FOR THE FAITH
> OF THE GOSPEL WITHOUT BEING FRIGHTENED
> IN ANY WAY BY THOSE WHO OPPOSE YOU.
> [PHILIPPIANS 1:27-28]

Our Rebellion is one reason why unity in the Church is so important. Opposition exists...and it seeks to divide us. Again, we're not at war with the culture, but we do refuse to go along with its assumptions and conclusions. We need each other's support in the thick of the friction this refusal inevitably creates.

And this friction needn't make us fearful. We can face threatening times together. Our shared faith in God can keep us calm and make us strong. Be thoughtful: Have I weakened the vitality of our cause by letting something unnecessarily divide me from a brother or sister in Christ?

> **THOUGH THERE SEEM TO BE FEW WITH US ON THIS NARROW WAY, WE WALK IT TOGETHER, JESUS WITH US.**

---WE PRAY---

"Spirit, I stand with my spiritual siblings with courage that comes from You."

THIS IS THE VERDICT: LIGHT HAS COME INTO THE WORLD, BUT PEOPLE LOVED DARKNESS INSTEAD OF LIGHT BECAUSE THEIR DEEDS WERE EVIL.
[JOHN 3:19]

What sets us apart as disciples of Jesus is that we have nothing to hide. Our non-conformity is best expressed by our transparency. We no longer have to put on our best face or pretend we're something we're not. We're real. We confess. We don't need to sweep our regrets under a rug; they're now trophies of God's grace.

Living in this clear, clean light is mutinous in a society obsessed with a carefully edited self-image. But it's only in such light we can truly see and show others the Way. Take a look around: Am I shading any areas of my heart and life to protect them from the light and keep them hidden in the dark?

> **IN A WORLD OF PRIDEFUL LYING AND HIDING, HONEST AND TRANSPARENT CONFESSION IS RADICAL.**

---WE PRAY---

"Lord, let me walk in the light, clear-minded and open-hearted."

9
KNOW BETTER

G. K. Chesterton was one of the great thinkers and writers of the twentieth century. In his book *Orthodoxy*, he described his journey to faith in Christ as a seafarer coming to port in his homeland while believing he was discovering a faraway shore.

Chesterton was highly educated and what they called in his day "a freethinker." Enjoying new ideas and always searching for a philosophy in which he could invest himself, he dismissed his native Christianity as surely holding little promise in his quest. But as he combed the moral and intellectual coastline, he realized the harbor he found most beautiful, useful, and admirable was actually the Way of Christianity. He wrote that he was a sailor who "discovered England under the impression that it was a new island in the South Seas."

He'd stumbled upon treasure by mistake, albeit a happy mistake. "What could be more delightful than to have in the same few minutes all the fascinating terrors of going abroad combined with all the humane security of coming home again?"[1] Faith in Jesus, His story and message, are, Chesterton discovered, in their bare and unadulterated goodness the highest and most nourishing truth there is—sturdy, enlivening, and ever-relevant. His revelation is one our world sorely needs. Author and historian John Dickson observes:

> Like Chesterton, many thoughtful folk have walked away from the religion associated with their childhood, or with childishness per se,

only to realize that some of their most mature "free thoughts" about justice, compassion, human rights, freedom, and so on are just an adult version of the Judeo-Christian worldview they thought they'd left behind.[2]

Like Chesterton sailing his intellectual high seas only to eventually admit his homeland was what'd he'd been searching for all along, we too can accept that Christianity actually does hold all the promise we need. Like the man in Jesus' parable (see Matthew 13:44) who finds treasure hidden in a field and sells all he has to purchase that field, so we can "discover" that our Christian faith is worth more—provides more, promises more—than anything else we have or ever could have. This is the "Eureka!" or "Aha!" or "lightbulb moment" everyone on the Way experiences. It's sublime.

We've been talking about walking the Way of Jesus and, in our tumultuous world, *keeping* to the ancient, beautiful, and ever-available Way of Jesus. Our doing so is a never-ending process which can be described in these three phases: Before saying yes to Christ we were 1) our Old Self on the Old Way. When we come to Christ, we enter new life. But there's still quite a bit of 2) our Old Self on the New Way. We still carry this with us as we're becoming 3) our New Self on the New Way, which is the goal of the Spirit's ongoing work in us.

Our Old Self is becoming our New Self while we walk this New Way. This is what it means to be a disciple of Jesus. We're *resisting* our old self and we're *rebelling* against the old way. Such rebellion means that **though we are deployed on this planet, we pledge our allegiance to our Father, who knows best.** He teaches us what we need to know, shows us the healthy and solid way to live, and enlists us in His mission to love everyone. Life in Him is far from lame or boring. It's infused with meaning.

We've received access to deeper knowledge. We understand.

It's not that we consider ourselves smarter than anyone else, but we can't deny that in Christ we are tapped into a deeper source, tuned into a stronger signal, of truth and reality. In God's Word and by His Spirit we simply perceive and understand things we couldn't perceive or understand before. We see this world as a God-bathed place dripping with significance.

Paul asked the Corinthian Christians these rhetorical questions: "Where is the wise person? Where is the teacher of the law? Where is the philosopher of this age? Has not God made foolish the wisdom of the world?" (1 Corinthians 1:20) He's creating a contrast here between what we used to consider wise—and what this world still considers so—and the wisdom of God. The first falls woefully short of the second.

What the world calls wisdom—what we might call conventional wisdom or more recently "the wisdom of crowds"[3] (a telling choice of words and an interesting concept within the marketplace, but dangerous as an approach to life since we know the crowded road is the one leading to destruction)—usually misses the point and even at its best scratches the surface. Indeed, it's usually pretty foolish. Think about it. Can any of us with a straight face look across the majority of our society today and take what we see and hear as a wise basis for living life and facing eternity? Would any of us conclude, "Yeah, looks like these folks have it figured out."? Everyone is struggling at best and pretty misguided on the whole. We observe this not self-righteously but matter-of-factly and with a heart to help.

> **BY MYSELF I DON'T HAVE MUCH FIGURED OUT EITHER, BUT I'M NO LONGER BY MYSELF. THAT'S THE POINT.**

Don't get me wrong, by myself I don't have anything figured out either. But I'm no longer by myself. That's the point. I've come to easily admit that I don't have the answers to the truly important questions, and so I lean on and learn from the One who does. Seeking knowledge by myself or believing that I and my fellow humans can discover and interpret all knowledge on our own is what leads to the empty and damaging worldviews of atheism (which yields a world void of absolute truth), humanism (which builds everything around us and our supposedly inevitable evolution), and narcissism (which removes all moral responsibility to our fellow humans). This is "the wisdom of the world." Our Rebellion is expressed in our belief that we are happily dependent upon God and that our wisest course of action is to make knowledge of Him our first aim.

Such dependence on a higher power for deeper knowledge is a counter-cultural posture today. Belief and faith are seen as discordant instead of harmonious with intelligence and reason. Dallas Willard refers to this in his book, *Hearing God*:

> Only a very hardy individualist or social rebel...stands any chance of discovering the substantiality of the spiritual life today. Today it is the skeptics who are the social conformists, though because of powerful intellectual propaganda they continue to enjoy thinking of themselves as wildly individualistic and unbearably bright.[4]

He observes that much of the beauty and truth of the spiritual life will go unnoticed by all except those ready to go against the flow of this world's thinking. Learning from Jesus isn't about intellectual passivity or disengaging our reason, but about mental fortitude and pressing through the haze of hollow, humanistic philosophies that pose as sagacity.

As long as our thinking begins with us, no matter how well-intentioned, we'll eventually steer off course, winding up at the wrong destination. We're smart, even brilliant at times, but not that brilliant. Not so bright we can outsmart God or leave Him behind in our evolved intelligence. "Do you see a person wise in their own eyes There is more hope for a fool than for them." (Proverbs 26:12) In our self-importance we become merely self-informed, which is—as life sooner or later proves to us—terribly inadequate.

> **AS LONG AS OUR THINKING BEGINS WITH US, NO MATTER HOW WELL-INTENTIONED, WE'LL EVENTUALLY STEER OFF COURSE.**

"What we have received is not the spirit of the world, but the Spirit who is from God," Paul wrote. And why have we received such a Spirit? "So that we may understand what God has freely given us." (1 Corinthians 2:12) As we leave the Old Way, and our Old Self becomes our New Self on the New Way, we begin to see things we couldn't see before. Our comprehension both expands and focuses, and we gain understanding. "The Holy Spirit, whom the Father will send in my name, will teach you all things," promised Jesus. (John 14:26)

So it is in consideration of this understanding that I want to take a moment and work through one of the most abused passages in all of Scripture today: the words of Jesus in Matthew 7:1, "Do not judge…"

Our society at large is in love with these three words, but let's consider them and their message in context. "Do not judge, or you too will be judged. For in the same way you judge others, you will be judged, and with the measure you use, it will be measured to you." (Matthew 7:1-2) Here Jesus is addressing our tendency to make ourselves the judge of others, assuming a role that belongs to God alone. He will indeed judge and is indeed the only One qualified to do so. Evaluating others is far from our primary calling. As I said in our initial chapters, our first and most important work is on our own character. We must spend our lives evaluating ourselves and asking God what needs to change in us.

> **JESUS KNOWS WE'RE QUICK TO FORGIVE, EXCUSE, OR OVERLOOK MOST OF OUR OWN SINS, BUT TOO EAGER TO HOLD AGAINST OTHERS THEIR SHORTCOMINGS.**

The easiest way to ignore our own need for maturity is to focus on the immaturity of others. Let's consider Jesus' next thoughts:

> Why do you look at the speck of sawdust in your brother's eye and pay no attention to the plank in your own eye? How can you say to your brother, 'Let me take the speck out of your eye,' when all the time there is a plank in your own eye? You hypocrite, first take the plank out of your own eye, and then you will see clearly to remove the speck from your brother's eye. (Matthew 7:3-5)

Jesus knows we're quick to forgive, excuse, or overlook most of our own sins, but too eager to hold against others their shortcomings. This is the spirit of a judgmental person placing themselves above another, thinking themselves qualified to pass judgment on the state or quality of another's soul, to *measure* them. Don't forget, Jesus exhorts us, that you're plank-eyed.

Nowhere is Jesus saying that the desire to help your brother or sister by removing a speck from their eye is a bad thing. (Who wants to keep a speck of anything in their eye?) Just don't pretend you don't need the same help. Taken together, these verses make it clear what Jesus is saying, and what He is not saying when he says, "Do not judge." Especially as we keep listening to Him in the verses ahead.

When we take the thought "do not judge"—as so many do today—to mean "do not use any moral discernment regarding others' behavior or make any distinctions between right and wrong, between wise and foolish practices," we are choosing to ignore the whole of Scripture's message because we are enamored by those three words, "Do not judge," and the supposed freedom and license they promote.

A few sentences later we read this admonition and foundational description of reality: "Enter through the narrow gate. For wide is the gate and broad is the road that leads to destruction, and many enter through it. But small is the gate and narrow the road that leads to life, and only a few find it." (Matthew 7:13-14) To simply follow Jesus' teaching here, we must be able to tell the difference between the broad and narrow roads and who is on them and what that means. And we have to call it for what it is. Doing so is not judging. It cannot be, for Jesus wouldn't instruct us to avoid the one and pursue the other if they were the same thing.

> **WE MUST BE ABLE TO TELL THE DIFFERENCE BETWEEN THE BROAD AND NARROW ROADS AND CALL IT FOR WHAT IT IS. DOING SO IS NOT JUDGING.**

He gives more guidance in the very next sentences. Hear His description of the discernment and, yes, wise judgment, His followers must exercise in the world. Read the words and remember they are spoken very shortly after the His warning, "Do not judge."

> Watch out for false prophets. They come to you in sheep's clothing, but inwardly they are ferocious wolves. By their fruit you will recognize them. Do people pick grapes from thornbushes, or figs from thistles? Likewise, every good tree bears good fruit, but a bad tree bears bad fruit. ...Every tree that does not bear good fruit is cut down and thrown into the fire. Thus, by their fruit you will recognize them.

Not everyone who says to me, "Lord, Lord," will enter the kingdom of heaven, but only the one who does the will of my Father who is in heaven. (Matthew 7:15-21)

Jesus is saying we must pay attention to others and their influence on us. That we must use discernment to decide if what they say is right or wrong, what they teach is good or bad. Are their words true or false? What is the fruit, the outcome, of their living?

All of this is difficult to digest for today's culture because it has cast aside most notions of objective morality and replaced it with a subjective—and frankly, impotent—form of tolerance as the highest ideal of morality. But it's a wrongly understood notion of tolerance. Tolerance used to rightly mean that one would respect another person even while having serious reservations about their ideas, worldviews, philosophies, or lifestyles. That's the whole idea of tolerance: that I will respect you, even love you, while I patiently tolerate our differences and incongruencies.

> **TODAY'S CULTURE HAS CAST ASIDE NOTIONS OF OBJECTIVE MORALITY AND REPLACED THEM WITH A SUBJECTIVE-AND IMPOTENT-FORM OF TOLERANCE.**

But today the concept of tolerance has been reoriented to mean that one must accept, embrace, and even celebrate every belief, every behavior, every creed. And anything less than this—any expression of disagreement, any recognition of substantive distinctions or differences in meaning—is considered today's worst sin of all: intolerance. There is no black and white today, only so many shades of grey. Everything is *right* and the only thing that's *wrong* is, of course, believing something is wrong. No one said such reasoning was reasonable. It's easy to see why "the wisdom of this world is foolishness in God's sight." (1 Corinthians 3:19)

Keepers of the Way see through this and exercise Spirit-enabled discernment as the Scriptures teach:

Stop judging by mere appearances, but instead *judge correctly*. (John 7:24, *emphasis* mine)

Don't let anyone deceive you in any way. (2 Thessalonians 2:3)

Test all things; hold fast what is good. Abstain from every form of evil. (1 Thessalonians 5:21-22)

Self-righteously evaluating another is condemned and rightly so, for it misses the point of love. However, the necessity and usefulness of making wise determinations about what's right and good and what is not is self-evident to any mature and well-functioning adult.

As followers of Jesus, we've received access to deeper knowledge, the kind that keeps us humble while filling us with truth. We understand now, we know better. And it's only as we know better that we can do better.

We've been called to a higher ethic. We obey.

When we "judge rightly" and "test all things" by the discernment given us by the Holy Spirit, we begin to see more and more clearly the Way of Jesus and match our way of life to it. Not so we can be better than others, but so we can be better. Finally better. We see the rightness and goodness of His ethic and we gladly obey it. Indeed, in obedience we find our gladness. As the psalmist wrote, "I run in the path of your commands. Teach me, LORD, the way of your decrees, that I may follow it to the end." (Psalm 119:32-33) We're not merely trudging, and there's no need to drag our feet.

> **WE SEEK TO MATCH OUR WAY OF LIFE TO THE WAY OF JESUS NOT SO WE CAN BE BETTER THAN OTHERS, BUT SO WE CAN BE BETTER. FINALLY BETTER.**

So what is this ethic? James put it memorably: "Religion that God our Father accepts as pure and faultless is this: to look after orphans and widows in their distress and to keep oneself from being polluted by the world." (James 1:27) Here we see James saying much the same as Paul said above: do good, abstain from worldliness.

Let's tag that concept on more time, this idea of abstaining from worldliness. It doesn't mean unplugging from modern technology or ignoring popular culture. That would be easy in the same way retreating to an enclave or eschewing automobiles and movie theaters is easy because it only addresses the externals of the issue. Instead, it simply but profoundly means not allowing our ways of thinking, living, prioritizing, behaving, and choosing be formed and informed by worldviews that refute or ignore biblical truth and the reality of Jesus. We live in the world, but we needn't—and mustn't—let the world live in us. As D.L. Moody once put it: "A ship lives in the water; but if the water gets into the ship, she goes to the bottom. So Christians may live in the world; but if the world gets into them, they sink."[5] And we need only spring a little leak.

Susanna Wesley had a tremendous grasp of this truth. She was a spiritual powerhouse who lived in the last half of the 1600s and the first half of the 1700s. She was the mother of 19 children, including John and Charles Wesley, whose influence on modern Christianity cannot be overstated. She wrote these words of advice to her young son, John:

> **IT'S NOT ABOUT THE KEEPING OF RELIGIOUS RULES AND PRECISE REGULATIONS. IT'S MUCH DEEPER, MORE GENUINE AND HONEST THAN THAT.**

> Whatever weakens your reason, impairs the tenderness of your conscience, obscures your sense of God, takes off your relish for spiritual things, whatever increases the authority of the body over the mind, that thing is sin to you, however innocent it may seem in itself.[6]

Whatever cools my spiritual fervor, whatever lulls me into choosing comfort over obedience, whatever blurs my perception of God's goodness and primacy, those things—whatever they may be and wherever in the world they are found—are sin to me. And my only reasonable response to them is resistance and rebellion. That's the mature point of view toward which we all should be aiming. It's not about the keeping of religious rules and precise regulations ("Just tell me what to do and what not to do and I'll keep to that list.") It's much deeper, more genuine and honest than that.

It's about the orientation of my heart and whether or not my character is growing to be more like Jesus. What that looks like for me and what it looks like for you won't be exactly the same, but when our heart orientation—and not merely externals—becomes what we most care about, we are tapping into the true meaning of what it means to be a Jesus-follower. As Paul summarized it to the Philippians: "Whatever happens, conduct yourselves in a manner worthy of the gospel of Christ." (Philippians 1:27) We're not managing our image so we'll pass the tests of others when they judge us; we're living transparently before Jesus for the glory of His Gospel. This is why we obey.

Disciples willingly, joyfully obey their Teacher and Master. It's inherent to the relationship. When Jesus commissioned His apostles to "make disciples," He said that meant baptizing and "teaching them to obey everything I have commanded you." (Matthew 28:19-20) Let's encounter our Master's words as though He is speaking them directly to us today...because He is. He's telling us not only how to make disciples but how to be ones.

> **TO KNOW HIM IS TO LOVE HIM.**
> **TO LOVE HIM IS TO OBEY HIM.**

Obedience is the difference. Obedience is Jesus' love language. "If you love me, keep my commands." (John 14:15) Jesus couldn't make it clearer: There's really no such thing as loving Jesus–or even believing in Him—without following His instruction, keeping His commands, obeying His teaching.

> Whoever has my commands and keeps them is the one who loves me. ...Anyone who loves me will obey my teaching. ...Anyone who does not love me will not obey my teaching. (John 14:21-24)
> If you keep my commands, you will remain in my love... (John 15:10)
> You are my friends if you do what I command. (John 15:14)

Are these the words of a power-hungry egotist? Perhaps they would be if they weren't spoken by the wisest, most integrated and graceful human ever, the perfectly holy and completely divine Son of God. To know Him is to love Him. To love Him is to obey Him. We don't love Him by merely believing in Him, but by living like Him.

Do I love Him? I want to. And often I do. But measured by my obedience I sometimes don't. I don't always keep His commands or obey His teaching. I don't always speak His love language. But when I do I know I am being my best and truest and self, satisfying my deepest longing and fulfilling my highest calling: I am His disciple, student, servant, and even friend. There's nothing else I'd rather be.

Ours is a rebellion fueled by truth, not image or attitude. We don't have chips on our shoulders, but crosses we're carrying. We see what's right and good and we begin—however imperfectly—to live according to it. We want to. God is a good Father; He knows best. We believe this to be true and real. This inevitably puts us at odds with the wisdom of the crowd and the ethics of the world. It also points us to a movement which demands our all.

We're enlisted in a greater cause. We sacrifice.

We not only begin to know better through our Spirit-envisioned understanding of Jesus' truth and our Spirit-enabled obedience to Jesus' ethic, we also gain a Spirit-empowered motivation for Jesus' mission. Paul wrote to Timothy: "No one serving as a soldier gets entangled in civilian affairs, but rather tries to please his commanding officer." (2 Timothy 2:4) What a perfect picture this gives us of life as followers of Jesus. The civilian world can come and go and do as it pleases, but we are enlisted men and women following the

> **THE CIVILIAN WORLD CAN COME AND GO AS IT PLEASES, BUT WE ARE ENLISTED MEN AND WOMEN FOLLOWING THE LAST STANDING ORDERS OF OUR COMMANDING OFFICER.**

last standing orders of our commanding officer, who happens to be the chief of every angel and the dread of every demon, the Lord of Hosts and the ruler of the armies of the Most High. And it is He who charges us to go into all this world and recruit more and more followers of His Way.

The life of those "serving as a soldier" is a life of sacrifice. "For it has been granted to you on behalf of Christ not only to believe in him, but also to suffer for him."(Philippians 1:29) For *Him*. Our cause is worth any suffering and sacrifice which accompany it because they are endured *for Him*. Recall the apostles elation after being flogged for sharing the Gospel: They were "rejoicing that God had counted them worthy to suffer disgrace for the name of

Jesus." (Acts 5:41) What fuels this joy that sees suffering for the cause of Christ as a privilege? The understanding that there is no greater cause. The apostles consistently expressed as much to the religious leaders seeking to shut them down. They knew to whom they reported, whose orders mattered:

> But Peter and John replied, "Which is right in God's eyes: to listen to you, or to him?" (Acts 4:19)
>
> Peter and the other apostles replied: "We must obey God rather than human beings!" (Acts 5:29)

In the Old Testament book of Daniel we read about young men who defied the laws of their pagan lands and refused to bow down to an idol as if it were God or pray to the king as if he were God. They rebelled under the threat of execution for non-compliance. I wonder, if the stories of Daniel chapters 3 and 6 were written today, what the people of God would be found bowing down to, found praying to, found putting their confidence in, found treating as if it were as important or as powerful as God. And if Christians today encountered situations like the apostles of Acts chapters 4 and 5, who would be found falling in line, quieting down, or playing it safe?

> **OUR CAUSE IS WORTH ANY SUFFERING OR SACRIFICE THAT ACCOMPANIES IT BECAUSE THEY ARE ENDURED FOR HIM.**

And I wonder who would be found refusing, found rebelling, found standing in that uncomfortable (if not illegal, at least counter-cultural) space in which obedience to God equals civil disobedience to this world. Not only believing in Him, but suffering—or at least sacrificing—for Him.

What does this look like? It's tutoring underprivileged kids so they can learn how to read. It's visiting the sick or taking a mission trip or giving sacrificially so your church family can reach more people. It's exercising creativity, making inspired art and music, and writing films, plays, and books. It's grieving the genocide of unborn generations and finding ourselves unable to celebrate the perversion of gender or the desecration of marriage. It's loving the hard-to-love and serving without hearing a "thank you." It's remembering those society forgets; it's supplying what the poor need. It's laughing with a child and crying with a veteran and sitting quietly with a widow.

It's keeping to the Way. It's what we do. Some of it merely costs us time, some of it can cost much more. All of it we pay gladly.

It was our friend and fellow traveler, G.K. Chesterton, who famously observed: "The Christian ideal has not been tried and found wanting. It has been found difficult; and left untried."[7] How true. For those who persevere, who join the Resistance, who fuel the Rebellion, who keep the Way, a trove of treasure awaits discovery: a deeper knowledge, a higher ethic, a greater cause. We must not give up or give in.

Pastor and author Mike Erre has written in *The Jesus of Suburbia: Have we tamed the Son of God to fit our lifestyle?* words that guide us well from the final thoughts of this section to the challenges of the next:

> If you follow Jesus, you follow the most radical man who ever existed. ...His is the most radical message you can preach or live. He turns everything upside down and calls us to do likewise. Jesus is not vitally committed to your comfort and safety; he is committed to the advance of his kingdom revolution in the hearts of people everywhere. ...The revolution of Jesus isn't for the faint of heart or the middle-of-the-road. It isn't safe. It isn't comfortable. It costs us a great deal to say yes. We take hold of the revolution by abandoning ourselves to Jesus and letting go of everything else.[8]

We let go of stuff, creature comforts and prestigious possessions. We let go of the opinions of others, of popularity and acceptance for their own sake. We let go of empty pursuits that cost us so much and accomplish so little.

Becoming our New Self and keeping to this New Way is the only thing that can make this world better, healthier, wiser. Changed people change the world. Our Resistance and Rebellion serve a greater result: Revolution.

WHERE IS THE PHILOSOPHER OF THIS AGE? HAS NOT GOD MADE FOOLISH THE WISDOM OF THE WORLD?
[1 Corinthians 1:20]

There's something we have to get used to if we're going to remain in this Rebellion as disciples of Jesus: being misunderstood by a culture that believes it has all the answers. It's a clash of worldviews...one that humbly accepts and celebrates God and His Word as the source of greatest wisdom, and one that proudly denies this and elevates us humans as the discoverers and purveyors of all knowledge.

Our forward thinking seems backward to the godless. Despite all their intelligence, they choose to live in ignorance of the realm of the soul and eternal truth. Any of us can know many things, but if we don't know God we are fools in the end.

Give it some serious thought: How easily can I be swayed by popular but groundless philosophies?

> **LEARNING IS GREAT, BUT WE SHOULD NEVER PROUDLY THINK OUR KNOWLEDGE CAN EXCEED GOD'S VAST WISDOM.**

---WE PRAY---

"God, I know nothing more worthwhile or more wise than Your Word."

> WHAT WE HAVE RECEIVED IS NOT THE SPIRIT OF
> THE WORLD, BUT THE SPIRIT WHO IS FROM GOD,
> SO THAT WE MAY UNDERSTAND WHAT
> GOD HAS FREELY GIVEN US.
> [1 CORINTHIANS 2:12]

Our Rebellion is fueled by our understanding that this world apart from Christ falls woefully short of supplying what we humans most need. God freely gives that to us: a purpose for our existence, grace for our fallenness, and power to live virtuously. By His Spirit we can see this. When we do, renouncing the ways of the world becomes a no-brainer.

But we don't always see it. The "spirit of the world" can be seductive and persuasive. We must remain filled with and focused on "the Spirit who is from God." Consider: With what am I filling myself today?

> **THROUGH GOD'S SPIRIT WE ARE ENLIGHTENED AND CAN SEE RIGHT THROUGH THE DIMNESS OF THIS WORLD.**

---WE PRAY---

"Spirit of God, only through You can I rightly understand what life is about."

> IT HAS BEEN GRANTED TO YOU ON BEHALF
> OF CHRIST NOT ONLY TO BELIEVE IN HIM,
> BUT ALSO TO SUFFER FOR HIM.
> [PHILIPPIANS 1:29]

Disciples of Jesus push against the magnetic pull of comfort and safety. The life of faith is inherently a life of some risk. We know that over the centuries it has been not at all uncommon for Christians to suffer inconvenience, injustice, mistreatment, persecution, and even violence because of their faith.

This is the price of our Rebellion. We don't buck the system without it exacting something from us. Why would Scripture so often encourage us to endure if there was no suffering to undergo? Take an inventory: What is my faith costing me? What have I had to endure because I'm a follower of Jesus?

> **OURS IS NOT A CASUAL BELIEF THAT COSTS US NOTHING, BUT A VISCERAL CONVICTION. CUT US AND WE BLEED JESUS.**

---WE PRAY---

"Christ, I'm blessed to believe in You and count it a gift to suffer for You."

> RELIGION THAT GOD OUR FATHER ACCEPTS AS PURE
> AND FAULTLESS IS THIS: TO LOOK AFTER ORPHANS
> AND WIDOWS IN THEIR DISTRESS AND TO KEEP
> ONESELF FROM BEING POLLUTED BY THE WORLD.
> [JAMES 1:27]

Our Rebellion doesn't spring from a juvenile need to do our own thing but from the God-given desire to do the right thing in a broken and wrong world. We're rebels with a cause. There's much good to be done here, and it begins with cultivating the good in us and guarding ourselves from the not-so-good.

Evangelist D.L. Moody once said that the Christian lives in the world much like a ship floats on the ocean. All is well until even a little bit of all that water starts flowing from outside to inside. Then things begin to sink. Check your levels: How much of the world's pollution is finding its way into me?

> **WE MUST GET OUR HANDS DIRTY IN SERVICE TO OTHERS, BUT KEEP OUR HEARTS UNSOILED IN DEVOTION TO GOD.**

---WE PRAY---

"God my Father, I want my faith to make a difference—in me and in others."

WHATEVER HAPPENS, CONDUCT YOURSELVES IN A MANNER WORTHY OF THE GOSPEL OF CHRIST.
[PHILIPPIANS 1:27]

Our Resistance and Rebellion isn't only about what we *don't* do or what we're against—far from it. We turn our lives *away* from the patterns and philosophies of this world because we're turning them *toward* the compelling, audacious Gospel of Christ. We're called to a cause worthy of all our best.

So in the midst of life's trials and this world's tests, we rise to the occasion and keep our courage up. We counter animosity with love. We face temptation with stubborn, Spirit-empowered determination. We do our life's work, whatever it may be, with joy and excellence. Ask yourself: What does the conduct of my life say about the Way of Jesus?

> **NO MATTER THE PRESSURE OF THIS WORLD'S PULL, WE KEEP OUR HANDS TO THE PLOW AND OUR EYES ON THE PRIZE.**

---WE PRAY---

"Christ, Your Gospel is worthy of my best effort and highest devotion."

No one serving as a soldier gets entangled in civilian affairs, but rather tries to please his commanding officer.
[2 Timothy 2:4]

Disciples of Jesus are members of an all-volunteer expedition force. We are clothed by Christ with His righteousness as our uniform. We are armed with the power of prayer, Scripture, and faith. And the last standing orders of our commanding officer are to take over the world with His love, grace, and truth.

So we live our lives with the focus and resolve of enlisted men and women. We do not live unto ourselves but as part of the corps. We have a mission. Our Resistance and Rebellion serve a greater cause: the Revolution. Consider: How potent would our movement be if every Christian were as engaged as I am? Or as entangled as I am?

> **WE KNOW TO WHOM WE ANSWER AND WHOSE ORDERS WE FOLLOW. OUR ALLEGIANCE IS CLEAR AND UNWAVERING.**

---WE PRAY---

"Jesus, enlist me in Your army to join Your mission of global takeover."

ADVANCE THE REVOLUTION

CHRIST'S LOVE COMPELS US
[2 CORINTHIANS 5:14]

10
LIGHT UP THE PLACE

Jesus started a revolution, not a religion. Perhaps you've heard or read that before and passed it off as a rhetorical flourish. Read it again at face value. It's true. Since it's true, we His followers must accept our responsibility to be revolutionaries, too.

Let me take us to the opening scene of Jesus' ministry. Speaking in His hometown synagogue, Jesus chooses these words from the prophet Isaiah as His inaugural address:

> The Spirit of the Lord is on me,
>   because he has anointed me
>   to proclaim good news to the poor.
> He has sent me to proclaim freedom for the prisoners
>   and recovery of sight for the blind,
> to set the oppressed free,
>   to proclaim the year of the Lord's favor. (Luke 4:18-19)

Words written centuries before which Jesus said apply to Him, were written about Him. "Today this scripture is fulfilled in your hearing," He concluded, essentially saying, "I am here to do what I just read." These were revolutionary words and a revolutionary claim. They were about something much more than mere religion.

Religion spends all its time determining who's in and who's out, instead of spending that same time trying to get people in. Religion spends all its effort making those on the inside feel comfortable, but Jesus was starting a revolution that would be dedicated to spreading God's love and good news to those on the outs.

Revolutions make religious people uncomfortable. And religious people can get very angry when they get uncomfortable. After making the claim we just read, Jesus began to explain its world-changing implications. What happened next seems like an epic-cool scene from a heroic action movie:

> **REVOLUTIONS MAKE RELIGIOUS PEOPLE UNCOMFORTABLE. AND BEING UNCOMFORTABLE CAN MAKE THEM VERY ANGRY.**

All the people in the synagogue were furious when they heard this. They got up, drove him out of the town, and took him to the brow of the hill on which the town was built, in order to throw him off the cliff. But he walked right through the crowd and went on his way. (Luke 4:28-30)

The Revolution had begun.

The cross was far from the first attempt of Jesus' life. These townspeople were ready to kill Jesus on Day One because He was announcing that things were about to change. Sight and freedom and good news for the blind and captive and poor—no matter who or where they are. (He's talking about you and me, let's not forget.) Jesus was setting in motion a love that would change the world. Pastor and author Vince Antonucci puts it perfectly:

> Jesus was a revolutionary, but his was a revolution of love. Revolutions tend to be about changing the power in a certain geographical territory, but the only geography that concerns Jesus is that of a person's soul. Jesus came to bring a revolution of the heart.[1]

As we begin talking about changing the world, we know it happens one heart at a time. The world gets changed through people, individual persons, changing.

And people are only truly, fully changed by the love of Jesus shown through you and through me. That's the basic equation of this whole enterprise.

When we hear or read the word *revolution*, we could easily replace it with *transformation*. Our never-changing God is absolutely all about change–changing our lives and changing the world. Christians who say they don't like or approve of change because "God never changes" are missing the point. He never changes because He doesn't need to; He's already perfect. However, you and I and everyone and everything else are far from perfect and perfectly qualified for change. And His change is always brought about through love.

Love is what the world most needs...and what turns it upside-down. That's what the first Christians were called: those who have turned the world upside-down. They advanced the Revolution. Let's talk about how that happens.

Love is a powerful seed that should not be stunted. It's time to grow.

"I will show you the most excellent way," (1 Corinthians 12:31) Paul said to the Corinthians. And then he began to describe and extol the virtues of love. He poetically wrote that any good we try to do which doesn't come from a place of love is no good at all in the end. Love's power cannot be overstated. As keepers of the Way we must never forget it is a Way of love, which is what makes it the "most excellent way."

> **ANY GOOD WE TRY TO DO THAT DOESN'T COME FROM A PLACE OF LOVE DOES NO GOOD AT ALL.**

Like a seed, it can seem small, even common. We use the word *love* all the time, referring to everything from the film we just watched, to pizza, to our kids, and to Jesus. But we can't let the ubiquity of the word or sentiment cause us to lose sight of love's true power. It is a tremendous force for change, in each of us and in this world. Indeed, "God is love." (1 John 4:16)

"Walk in the way of love, just as Christ loved us and gave himself up for us as a fragrant offering and sacrifice to God." (Ephesians 5:2) Just as Christ gave Himself up, we give ourselves up. When speaking to His disciples of His impending death Jesus described His choice as like planting a seed and called them to the same sacrifice:

The hour has come for the Son of Man to be glorified. Very truly I tell you, unless a kernel of wheat falls to the ground and dies, it remains only a single seed. But if it dies, it produces many seeds. Anyone who loves their life will lose it, while anyone who hates their life in this world will keep it for eternal life. (John 12:23-25)

Like a seed that dies when it is planted, so He gave His life and planted His love in us. We must let it grow. "This is how we know what love is: Jesus Christ laid down his life for us. And we ought to lay down our lives for our brothers and sisters." (1 John 3:16) This is what it means to be a keeper of the most excellent Way of love.

Just as Jesus said that it's only as a seed is planted that it can transform into something else, we let His love be planted in us so we may grow strong and mature, transformed into something fruitful. This growth means becoming more and more expert at this thing called love. It's difficult to be sure; there are lots of twists and turns and tough decisions sometimes made in tough love, plenty of occasions for patience and forgiveness and sometimes simply putting up with others. But it's all love all the same. We orient our hearts toward love. We ask God to fill our hearts with love. And when we can allow ourselves, submit ourselves to love others, we find ourselves becoming changed people who change the world, who advance the Revolution of Jesus. Like a seed growing and spreading its roots with a persistence that can upheave sidewalks and structures, ours is a quiet, humble insurgency.

> **LIKE ROOTS THAT SPREAD WITH A PERSISTENCE THAT CAN UPHEAVE SIDEWALKS AND STRUCTURES, OURS IS A QUIET, HUMBLE INSURGENCY.**

Shane Claiborne, a Christian author and activist known for his work with the poor of Philadelphia, has described his view of our calling this way:

> The revolution will not be televised. It will not be brought to you by Fox News with commercial interruptions. ...It will not be sandwiched between ads to accelerate your life or be all you can be. There will be

no reruns. The revolution will be live. The revolution will be cleaning toilets and giving another blanket. ...The revolution will not be talking about poverty in hotel banquet rooms. It will be eating beans and rice... Get ready, friends...God is preparing us for something really, really—small.[2]

We can tend to miscalculate the weight of our meager assistance or the value of our modest service. But it's those seemingly insignificant acts, when done in love, we realize aren't insignificant at all. Not to God, and certainly not to their recipients. Ever receive an act of love from another and think, "That was a rather small thing. I'm not sure how I feel about that. I bet they could've done better."? I doubt it. We love to be loved. And we delight to see others' love tanks get filled, showing them they are such valuable and vibrant souls on this earth. This is what love does.

> **WE DELIGHT TO SHOW OTHERS THEY ARE SUCH VALUABLE AND VIBRANT SOULS ON THIS EARTH. THIS IS WHAT LOVE DOES.**

Ours is a quiet, steady revolution, but a revolution nonetheless. Remember how some early Christians were described by the rioting mob of Thessalonians as they searched for Paul and Silas:

> And when they could not find them, they dragged Jason and some of the brothers before the city authorities, shouting, "These men who have *turned the world upside down* have come here also, and Jason has received them, and they are all acting against the decrees of Caesar, saying that there is another king, Jesus." (Acts 17:6-7 ESV)

This phrase "turned the world upside down" is elsewhere translated: to start an uproar or a revolt, to agitate. The Bible's New International Version puts it this way: "These men who have caused trouble all over the world have now come here." Just as the townspeople of Nazareth were not happy with Jesus (to say the least), so the citizens of Thessalonica were unhappy with these Jesus-followers. How dare they buck the system, not fall in line with Caesar, claim there is another, greater king! They were the very definition of audacious. Their disregard for convention or authority, much less personal safety, was an affront to the norm that could not be ignored.

Now friend, let us declare today there indeed is another King. You bet there is. His name is Jesus. He's the King of all, an everlasting king. He's the King of my life and I pray He's the King of yours. We're called to simply live in that reality, to live out that beautiful, powerful truth as happy citizens of His good kingdom. This will inevitably flip over some things people hold sacred and upset some people's vested interests in the status quo. So be it.

May we follow in these blessedly dangerous footsteps. May we be seen as holy and humble troublemakers who turn worlds upside down with the love of our King Jesus. It's a revolution that could not be stopped because love cannot be stopped, a powerful seed that should not be stunted. It's time to let it grow and spread and takeover the kingdoms of this world.

Love is a shining light that cannot be hidden. It's time to glow.

Growing up in church, I remember singing as a child, "This little light of mine, I'm gonna let it shine." Jesus said we don't merely *have* a light *to shine*—we *are* a light *that shines*. "You are the light of the world. A town built on a hill cannot be hidden. Neither do people light a lamp and put it under a bowl. Instead they put it on its stand, and it gives light to everyone in the house." (Matthew 5:14-15) Followers of Jesus illuminate the world, spreading life-giving light to "everyone in the house" so they needn't sit in darkness any longer. This brightness is, of course, not from ourselves or our intelligence, but from Christ and His wisdom in us.

> JESUS SAID WE DON'T MERELY HAVE A LIGHT TO SHINE— WE ARE A LIGHT THAT SHINES.

This image of you and I as a lit lamp or torch is a useful one for us. It is the natural—and I think most powerful—outcome of where we started this book: tend to your own character, the fire of your own heart and soul, and let it burn brightly. Healthy and potent things will flow from that. This internal work is our first and most essential—and interestingly, our most externally effectual— work.

What we're talking about here is so simple that we understand it as children. Glowing is an organic thing. Jesus is saying that as a light naturally glows, so can—and should—we. As the song declares, we don't force or muster light to shine; we *let it shine*. As D.L. Moody once said, "We are told to let our light shine, and if it does, we won't need to tell anybody it does. Lighthouses don't fire cannons to call attention to their shining—they just shine."[3]

We allow ourselves to simply be what and who we are in Jesus. Our be-ing, before and above our do-ing, has a brilliant influence in this world. We mustn't hide who we are, keeping ourselves "under a bowl." (The implication in Jesus' words is that no one would do such a thing.) And we must never underestimate the power of even a little light.

It's the power of contrast, of highlighting the difference—sometimes stark—between one thing and another. Our lives can have just such power as we demonstrate the uniqueness of life lived in Christ. Not surprisingly, the Scriptures repeatedly describe this contrast as the relationship of light and darkness. Paul did in his letter to the Ephesians:

> **OUR BE-ING, BEFORE AND ABOVE OUR DO-ING, HAS A BRILLIANT INFLUENCE IN THE WORLD.**

> For you were once darkness, but now you are light in the Lord. Live as children of light (for the fruit of the light consists in all goodness, righteousness and truth) and find out what pleases the Lord. Have nothing to do with the fruitless deeds of darkness, but rather expose them. (Ephesians 5:8-11)

Those pursuits which are pointless and dim—the fruitless deeds of darkness—are easily seen for the worthless works they are in the light of lives humbly lived for the Lord. We "expose them" not through harsh judgments or finger-wagging accusations, but simply by being the "children of the light" we are and letting that illumination cast the contrast.

We are calling people to a life—not a system or an organization or a culture, but a life we're actually living. On this point Dallas Willard is worth quoting at length:

The revolution of Jesus is first and always a revolution of the human heart. His revolution does not proceed through the means of social institutions and laws—the outer forms of our existence... Rather, his is a *revolution of character*, which proceeds by changing people from the inside through ongoing personal relationship with God and one another. It is a revolution that changes people's ideas, beliefs, feelings, and habits of choice, as well as their bodily tendencies and social relations. It penetrates to the deepest layers of their soul. External, social arrangements may be useful to this end, but they are not the end, nor are they a fundamental part of the means.[4]

> **BEING AND BECOMING OUR BEST AND FULLEST SELVES... THIS ALONE IS MORE IMPACTFUL THAN WE THINK.**

This is the Revolution that's taken place in us. To this we call others. It is a tremendous privilege to do so, though often we can get confused regarding the call. (We may ask people to be merely moral or politically conservative or traditionally church-going, instead of asking them to follow Jesus.) Sometimes we're less-than-convinced we ourselves even have something worth sharing.

Don't underestimate the amount of influence and the degree of impact you can have in this world by fully being you, a sincere, heartfelt, passionate, joyful, loving, wise, winsome disciple of Jesus. Catherine of Siena once said, "Be who God meant you to be and you will set the world on fire."[5] Be yourself, the self Christ is recreating and transforming, the self God had in mind when He designed you and decided you should be. Being and becoming our best and fullest selves...this alone is more impactful than we think. "Hide it under a bushel? No! I'm gonna let it shine."

LOVE IS A RELENTLESS FORCE THAT MUST NOT BE PASSIVE. IT'S TIME TO GO.

I'm sure you've noticed a progression here. Love grows in us like a seed. It produces a wellness in us that gives us a healthy glow. This energy swells within us and moves us forward, makes us go. "Christ's love compels us." (2

Corinthians 5:14) It's at this point we realize that while we can act without love, we cannot love without action. When we see the world and its need, we are compelled to respond. Love is that response. "Let's not merely say that we love each other; let us show the truth by our actions." (1 John 3:18 NLT)

Our be-ing is always the beginning, to be sure, but it's our do-ing that wins the day. "The only thing that counts is faith expressing itself through love." (Galatians 5:6) Love is what gives us a heart for the lost, motivates us to witness to others, to risk the conversation, to get personally involved in our community, to invest our resources. Love requires work and service. And no love revolution can begin in and through us until we are ready to forego our own comfort in love's labor. We have to get off our couches. We have to get uncomfortable. We have to let love *move us*.

Repeatedly in the Gospels we read of Jesus being moved with compassion (see Matthew 14:14, Mark 1:41, Luke 7:13). The Greek word is *splagchnizomai* which literally means *to be moved in your intestines*. Back then, the seat of love and emotion was not imagined to be the heart, but the bowels. So when Jesus saw a harassed crowd or a blind beggar or a grieving widow, He felt it in His gut. Love moved Him. And He walked into, not away from, the pain of others. As we seek to be like Him, this is instructive. We must let love move and compel us. We must make compassion our compass. That's certainly what the earliest Waykeepers did.

> **WE MUST LET LOVE MOVE AND COMPEL US. WE MUST MAKE COMPASSION OUR COMPASS.**

The Church grew rapidly between the years of 100 and 300 AD. Historians who study this say two of the biggest drivers to this growth were two major plagues which swept through that area of the world. In some cities, two-thirds of the population died. In 251 AD, at the height of one of these plagues, five thousand people were dying every day.

When the plagues came, everyone fled the cities to escape the lethal contagion—everyone, that is, except Christians, who stayed and ministered to the sick and dying. Everyone else was running away from the pain, the Jesus-followers ran toward it. Dionysius, then Bishop of Alexandria, wrote how the Christians responded to the plague of 250 AD. He explains they...

showed unbounded love and loyalty, never sparing themselves and thinking only of one another. Heedless of danger, they took charge of the sick, attending to their every need and ministering to them in Christ, and with them departed this life serenely happy; for they were infected by others with the disease, drawing on themselves the sickness of their neighbors and cheerfully accepting their pains. Many, in nursing and curing others, transferred their death to themselves and died in their stead.[6]

Most of the time, most of us want to avoid whatever's messy or risky, unless the risk or mess must be endured for the people we love. That's different. And how Jesus makes us different is that now the circle of who we love is—prayerfully—ever-expanding and all-inclusive. A plague can certainly be understood as a situation of ultimate avoidance. But these Christians leaned into the pain, ran to the need while others fled. They knew they had joined a revolution, not a religion. In a place of contagious death they brought contagious life and the Revolution spread because of it.

> **LOVE MUST BE LEARNED, AND LEARNED AGAIN. THERE IS NO END TO THESE LESSONS IF ONE IS WILLING TO LEARN.**

Today countless souls suffer a plague of ambivalence and often hatred, a famine of love. As we heard Mother Teresa observe in our first chapter: "There are many in the world who are dying for a piece of bread but there are many more dying for a little love." This harsh world is full of people who desperately need to be loved. Some know it; some don't and try to fill their need for real love with other things: the next party, the next hit, buzz, or thrill, the next relationship, outfit, gadget, vacation, or car, a new project, new book, new game, or new movie. But what they need is love. God knew this world would leave people broken and hungry for love. The good thing—the so very, very good thing—is, He is love.

Love must be learned, and learned again. There is no end to these lessons if one is willing to learn, willing to remain enrolled in the school of our Rabbi, who is love incarnate. We ought to be experts at love, or at least aiming to be, not because we're so innately smart and selfless, but because True Love lives in us. This is what causes John to ask so emphatically, "If anyone…sees his brother in need, yet closes his heart against him, how does God's love abide in him?" (1 John 3:17 ESV) Here we find that especially telling Greek word in its noun form: *splagchnon.* The King James Version more explicitly translates John's question: If one sees another in need and "shutteth up his bowels of compassion from him, how dwelleth the love of God in him?" The implication is clear: The Way of love is open-hearted, and those who keep to it will be consistently moved to action, serving and meeting the needs of others in Jesus' Name. *Loving* is an action verb in a big way.

This means our Revolution looks a lot like hard work, which is an intrinsic part of the Christian life. Not empty works to earn God's favor, but full-throttled exertion to fulfill His mission. It is apparent from His teaching that Jesus believed life in the kingdom is a life of labor.

> In the parable of the workers in the vineyard, Jesus said, "For the kingdom of heaven is like a landowner who went out early in the morning to hire men to work in his vineyard." (Matthew 20:1) He hires more workers throughout the day and pays them all the same wage at day's end. It matters not how long you've worked, Jesus emphasized, but that you went to work when you heard the call.

> **THE WAY OF LOVE IS OPEN-HEARTED, AND THOSE WHO KEEP TO IT WILL BE CONSISTENTLY MOVED TO ACTION, MEETING OTHERS' NEEDS IN JESUS' NAME.**

> In another parable (Matthew 21:29-32), a father asks his son to go work in the vineyard. One says yes and then neglects to go. The other refuses and then later gets to work. In Jesus' eyes it wasn't the right words of the first, but the right actions of the second that counted.

> At one point, Jesus spoke about His second coming and describes the owner of a house leaving, but with plans to return. "He…puts his servants in charge, each with his assigned task… You do not know

when the owner of the house will come back...do not let him find you sleeping." (Mark 13:32-37)

Jesus prepared a would-be disciple: "No one who puts his hand to the plow and looks back is fit for service in the kingdom of God." (Luke 9:62) Ever been behind a plow? It's hard work. But isn't it interesting that this is the picture Jesus gave of being His disciple: a plow hand? But we shouldn't be surprised. Remember what He said in Luke 10:2: We aren't tourists or picnickers in the harvest field, we're *laborers*.

I could go on with more examples, but it's easy to see that when Jesus considers His followers, He thinks of hands on plows, of get down to our Father's business, nitty-gritty work done by laborers and servants. And he counts Himself among them. His final charge to His apostles was to "go," assuring them He was going with them (see Matthew 28:18-20).

Jesus said such going would be the evidence and result of our glowing, that one would translate to the other. "Let your light shine before others, that they may see your good deeds and glorify your Father in heaven." (Matthew 5:16) Good deeds driven not by obligation or the need to appear righteous, but by well-lit love that glows and goes and draws people to God. This is the force we're called to exert in the world, the engine of our revolutionary faith.

I'm convinced there are ministries and non-profits in embryo in so many of us, quite probably in you as you read this book. Organizations and movements ready to be birthed. Great differences ready to be made. People to be fed, futures to be changed. Screenplays to be written and sculptures to be formed. I believe there is awakened within each of us as Christ-followers a source of creativity that has the capacity to change hearts and captivate minds. That's the amazing thing about the Church: As the love of Christ flows *to* each of us, it flows *through* each of us to others in a beautiful diversity of expressions.

> **AWAKENED WITHIN EACH OF US AS CHRIST-FOLLOWERS IS A SOURCE OF CREATIVITY WITH THE CAPACITY TO CHANGE HEARTS AND CAPTIVATE MINDS.**

Perhaps compassion moves you toward the sick, perhaps the homeless. Maybe you're called to teach children or comfort the grieving or financially support missionaries. When Christ's love compels you, the first people you think of may be the imprisoned, or returning veterans, or single parents. Whatever this looks like for you, *go for it*. That's how the world gets changed. We must say yes, and keep saying yes, to all Christ has for us, letting ourselves be filled with Him so we can be emptied for others. Ready to sacrifice and serve, to pour ourselves out, ready to go and go and go.

> **WE MUST SAY YES, AND KEEP SAYING YES, TO ALL CHRIST HAS FOR US, LETTING OURSELVES BE FILLED WITH HIM SO WE CAN BE EMPTIED FOR OTHERS.**

Faith in Jesus doesn't just get us glowing, it gets us going. We're made to move. Revolutions aren't known for their inaction or mere aspiration. Quite the contrary. Our faith must move beyond mere ideas and ideals, concepts and creeds. Real faith does stuff, get's stuff done. James stated it bluntly: "Faith by itself, if it is not accompanied by action, is dead." (James 2:17)

Before I close this chapter, there is one more point to make. With all this talk of love, even revolutionary love, the tragic fact is so many of us don't love because we're not truly convinced we are loved. We love the thought of being loved, but we haven't let the reality of it really soak in. Brennan Manning has written well what I want to convey:

> When I have not had the experience of being loved by God, just as I am and not as I should be, then loving others becomes a duty, a responsibility, a chore. But if I let myself be loved as I am, with the love of God poured into my heart by the Holy Spirit, then I can reach out to others in a more effortless way.[7]

That's right. This Way, while being one of serious labor, is also effortless. In other words, love's gotta flow. We give only what we've received. Remember, it's only changed people who change the world. So let me remind you whether you need reminded or not: You are completely loved by our Father God. Today, right now. So let yourself be loved.

Whatever you've done or others have done to you, whatever has happened to you, whatever is part of your story up to today...God knows every detail. He may be grieved by some of it, but He's surprised by none of it. And not a single aspect or moment of that story has diminished His love for you. Not at all, not in the slightest.

Maybe you'll close this book and walk back into your messy life—messy relationally, financially, spiritually. He wants to turn that upside down and bring some order. That's His love revolution in you.

Maybe your life is neat and clean, a place for everything and everything in its place—organizationally, even emotionally and spiritually. He wants to turn that upside down and get messy. That's His love revolution for you.

He wants to turn our hurt upside down into forgiveness, our anger into passion. He wants to turn our me-centered way of living into an others-centered life of giving.

Love is how it all begins. Love is the means and love is the ends. Love lights up the place.

I WILL SHOW YOU THE MOST EXCELLENT WAY.
[1 CORINTHIANS 12:31]

The only way we'll change this world is through love. Our love for God and His love in us deepens and expands our love for others. As the passage quoted above makes clear: We may share God's truth with great volume or eloquence, but if our delivery is without love it does more harm than good.

One word at a time, one act of service and gesture of caring at a time, we can change the world one man, woman, and child at a time. Remember: "Love is patient..." (1 Corinthians 13:4) This Revolution is a steady, relentless overthrow of darkness with light, of guilt with grace, of ignorance with wisdom. The question we each must ask ourselves is: Am I ready to live my faith not only as an internal salvation but as an external mission?

> **WHAT THIS WORLD NEEDS MOST IS LOVE-REAL LOVE THAT COMES FROM THE ORIGINAL AND HIGHEST LOVER.**

---WE PRAY---

"Lord, Your love is the greatest force on earth. May it be strong in me."

Walk in the way of love, just as Christ loved us and gave himself up for us as a fragrant offering and sacrifice to God.
[Ephesians 5:2]

Jesus started this Revolution; we are only carrying it forward. He taught, He served, He loved to the extreme. We follow in His footsteps as an army of people willingly giving our lives away every day and in everyday ways for the good of others.

We Christians are the ones who should lead the world in love, showing the world what love truly looks like. We've found what everyone's looking for. As John explains in his first letter, "This is how we know what love is: Jesus Christ laid down his life for us. And we ought to lay down our lives for our brothers and sisters." (3:16) Consider: When was the last time I loved another to the point of serious sacrifice?

> **LIKE OUR LORD, WE LOVE OTHERS LIBERALLY TO THE POINT OF SACRIFICING OURSELVES FOR THEIR GOOD.**

---WE PRAY---

"Christ, help me walk as You walked in the way of sacrificial love."

THESE MEN WHO HAVE CAUSED TROUBLE ALL OVER THE WORLD HAVE NOW COME HERE.
[ACTS 17:6]

In various translations of the above scripture, these early Christians are described as those who *have turned the world upside down*, *have been disturbing the peace*, and *have subverted the state of the world*. These phrases get to the heart of what was happening. In the original language the same verb, which means "to stir up, excite, or unsettle," is used twice in this single sentence.

The point? Where disciples of Jesus go, things don't stay the same. The status quo is disrupted. Old orders are upset. What's accepted as normal is brought into question. The Good News *is news*, and news means new, means change. Ask yourself: What change do I bring with me wherever I go?

> **THIS WORLD CAN GET UPSIDE DOWN AND BACKWARDS. OUR WORK IS TO SET IT RIGHT AGAIN, ONE HEART AT A TIME.**

—WE PRAY—

"Lord, wherever I go may my arrival make a difference for You."

In the same way, faith by itself, if it is not accompanied by action, is dead.
[James 2:17]

Beneficial change and healthy progress don't happen by accident. Doing good is proactive, not passive. Somehow some of us have fallen for the idea that Christianity is merely about belief, only about agreeing with the correct creed.

Right belief is essential but not enough. Ours is a belief about which it is impossible to be idle. It's too compelling, too revolutionary. If we say we believe in the message of Jesus but do nothing to engage in His mission, we reveal we don't really understand what we say we believe. A faith that's alive is a faith that *moves*. Take your pulse: Is my faith alive and not dead? Is it accompanied by prayerful action?

> **WE SIMPLY CAN'T CLAIM TO BELIEVE IN JESUS AND THEN DO NOTHING TO SPREAD HIS MESSAGE AROUND THE WORLD.**

—— WE PRAY ——

"Father, may my faith in You move me to act and make an impact."

You are the light of the world. A town built on a hill cannot be hidden.
[Matthew 5:14]

When Jesus tells us what we are, we are wise to listen and believe Him. He says His followers are a light by which this world can see. Like a hilltop town under the night sky, our glow cannot be missed. Warm and welcoming, the Church is a beacon guiding weary travelers to shelter.

So we mustn't hold back or hide who we are. "Now you are light in the Lord. Live as children of light..." (Ephesians 5:8) Revolutionaries aren't known for their reserve. And humility does not equal timidity. Contemplate this: Do I believe the Spirit's presence in me means I have something illuminating to offer the world?

> **AS WE GENUINELY AND HUMBLY FOLLOW JESUS, THE EVIDENCE OF HIS PRESENCE IN US BECOMES UNDENIABLE.**

---WE PRAY---

"Holy Spirit, light me up and glow through me."

> LET YOUR LIGHT SHINE BEFORE OTHERS,
> THAT THEY MAY SEE YOUR GOOD DEEDS
> AND GLORIFY YOUR FATHER IN HEAVEN.
> [MATTHEW 5:16]

When we resolve to be the light Jesus says we are, our good work in the world will point people to God. That's how we shine. These shiny deeds aren't to highlight how good we are, but how good God is in us. And they come in many forms: kindness to a stranger, patience with a child, endurance through a trial, generosity to someone in need. Our Revolution is nothing if not the aggregation of countless consistent good deeds done out of love for Jesus.

Light is meant to shine, and when we let Jesus shine through us it will not go unnoticed. Don't overthink it: What glowing good deed can I do today to shed light onto the path to God?

> **THIS WORLD IS LOOKING FOR A TRUTH THAT'S SPOKEN NOT ONLY IN WORDS, BUT EVEN MORE POTENTLY IN ACTION.**

---WE PRAY---

"Heavenly Father, may others see You through the good I choose to do."

ADVANCE THE REVOLUTION

11
SEND A MESSAGE

One of this book's primary themes is that the Way of Christ we follow today is an ancient and beautiful path which Christians before us have followed for nearly two millennia, and that in today's modern and postmodern American culture it can feel as though some of this beauty and meaning are lost, or at least lost on us. It can be easy to forget that behind and underneath whatever current expressions of Christianity and the Church we see (many wonderful, some disappointing, too many disheartening) is a vital truth and energy, like a robust river unstoppably flowing through the last twenty centuries of human history and culture. But when we forget this, we lose a lot.

So in light of that, let me tell you about a document that until the 1880s scholars had only read about but had never seen or read themselves. It's called *The Teaching of the Apostles* or *The Didache* (<u>did</u>-a-kay)—Greek for *teaching*. It's a second-generation Christian writing, kind of a handbook written late in the first century for Gentile disciples of Jesus .

Christians in the second and third centuries wrote about and referred to *The Didache*, but until a copy was discovered in 1883, no one in modern times had ever laid eyes on it. This writing teaches about ethics, baptism, fasting and prayer, communion, and resurrection. But I want to call our attention to how it begins, how it lays out the reality of what it means to be a follower of Jesus the Christ. Here's the first line of text: "There are two Ways: a Way of Life and a Way of Death, and the difference between these two Ways is great."[1]

Friend, we've spent our first ten chapters staking this same claim: There is a Way of life that's the Way *to* Life and we are keeping to it and keepers of it. And now we explore what it means to stand on that Way today and consider our call to change the world by calling others to this Way. We will see **we are sent on a mission to rescue others, not refute or reject them.**

So often we Christians can get this backwards. We lend our two cents instead of leading a hand. We look to win arguments instead of seeking to win souls. We love people, but mostly the ones who love us back. These are no ways to change the world, which—let's be clear—is exactly what we're sent to do.

WE ARE SENT AS JESUS WAS SENT, WITH BOTH GRACE AND TRUTH.

Ours is a faith of tensions that calls us to keep our grip on dualities because reality is never as simple as we would prefer. One of the most important and most challenging of these tensions is the one that exists (or can seem to exist) between grace and truth.

John's initial description of Jesus immediately embraces such tension and mystery: "The Word became flesh and made his dwelling among us. We have seen his glory, the glory of the one and only Son, who came from the Father, full of grace and truth." (John 1:14) Navigating this tension was effortless for Jesus because He could completely comprehend—indeed, He embodied—how grace and truth work together. Only as we become more like Him can we understand this too. As we walk with others through life on this earth, we seek to embody grace and truth. It starts in us. We're called to get a good grip on realities that at first may seem contradictory, but ultimately we realize are complementary. Truth says, "I'm accountable for my actions." While grace says, "But you're also forgiven." Both are correct. Grace says, "It is well." Truth says, "No, you're broken." Both are right. Grace says, "God will take care of it." Truth says, "Oh, you're going to have to work on it." Both are accurate.

> **OURS IS A FAITH THAT CALLS US TO KEEP OUR GRIP ON DUALITIES BECAUSE REALITY IS NEVER AS SIMPLE AS WE PREFER.**

Send a Message

And so the more clearly we see ourselves as sent into this world as Jesus was sent, the more confidently we can hold these tensions together for ourselves. Which readies us to be agents of that same change in the world around us.

As Jesus said to Nicodemus, "For God did not send his Son into the world to condemn the world, but to save the world through him." (John 3:17) If that's true of Jesus, it should become true of us as His followers He has sent. We can tell others the truth about Jesus, including what's right and good and what's not, in a way that's not condemning of them as persons God loves. Indeed, you've never laid eyes on, never bumped into anyone God does not know and love.

So we take up Jesus' same mission: to save and not condemn. What does this look like, to be people sent to share Jesus' salvation and do so without adding condemnation? In our words and actions, our tone and our posture with others, we convey, "I'm not going to pretend I've got it all perfectly together. I'm also not going to pretend that this or that thing is right, healthy, or wise when God has made it clear it's not." We have a lot of such redefinition going on in our world today.

> **GRACE COMES TO US FREELY AND BEAUTIFULLY WITH ARMFULS OF TRUTH AS WELCOME HOME PRESENTS.**

But the bigger point is we're all wrong in our own ways. "I'm not here to condemn you. I condemned myself by ignoring God. Then He—I came to understand—came to my rescue. And I've only discovered what's right and good through Him, not by any virtue of my own. I'm wrong, you're wrong, we're all kinds of wrong. Only Jesus can set us right." Grace comes to us freely and beautifully with armfuls of truth as our "welcome home" presents.

You see, people can say and do whatever they want concerning a variety of issues, and argue about any number of things, but when their heads hit their pillows each night, to what conclusions do they arrive concerning this world and how it came to be and their own human consciousness and eternity and who they are in this universe? Until an individual is ready to confront the question, "What am I going to do about God and my soul?" then our job is to love them with grace and truth. Until such questions are ready to be addressed, debating about peripheral issues doesn't save anybody, doesn't change anyone's hearts or minds. Only proper introductions to Jesus can ever do that. Our job is love them and get them to Him. Do we really think change will come to them any other way?

Praying to the Father about His disciples, Jesus stated plainly, "As you sent me into the world, I have sent them into the world." (John 17:18) We're not incorrect to apply those words to ourselves as modern-day disciples. That's us too: sent into the world. Can we accept the idea we weren't just born here, but sent here? Sent by God to our time and place? Sent for others?

To answer in the affirmative speaks of a purpose and a meaning and a drive that gets us out of bed each morning with more than a little focus and energy. Mother Teresa said as much in a speech at Cambridge University:

> And today God keeps on loving the world, He keeps on sending you and me to prove that He loves the world, that He still has that compassion for the world. It is we who have to be His Love, His compassion in the world of today. But to be able to love we must have faith, for faith in action is love, and love in action is service.[2]

DEBATING PERIPHERAL ISSUES CAN'T CHANGE ANYONE'S HEART. ONLY PROPER INTRODUCTIONS TO JESUS CAN EVER DO THAT.

Wouldn't it be great if what the world thought of the Church is what we hear Mother Teresa saying: that the Church is proof God loves the world? What a joyous thing it would be if the world could genuinely exclaim, "God must still love us, look at these amazing people He has sent to share with us His love!" Brothers and sisters, can we live into that and up to that? I know we can.

WE ARE SENT AMIDST THREAT, BUT WITH POWER AND STRATEGY.

The world into which we are sent presents to us an unpredictable combination of opposition and opportunity. As Jesus' followers, we do well to remind ourselves of His thoughtful choice of words as He deployed (and deploys) His disciples:

> I am sending you out like sheep among wolves. Therefore be as shrewd as snakes and as innocent as doves. Be on your guard; you will be handed over to the local councils and be flogged in the synagogues. On my account you will be brought before governors and kings as witnesses to them and to the Gentiles. But when they arrest you, do not worry about what to say or how to say it. At that time you will be given what to say, for it will not be you speaking, but the Spirit of your Father speaking through you. (Matthew 10:16-20)

> **WE CAN BE GOOD WITHOUT BEING GULLIBLE, INNOCENT BUT NOT IGNORANT.**

Jesus is adeptly advising His disciples and, by extension, you and me today. We are sent into a world that makes us seem like sheep among wolves. There are some ravenous threats we face out there, but Jesus assures we're far from alone, and that by His Spirit we can handle it. He promises we will be endowed with confidence and the courage to speak the truth.

On account of Me, when My name comes up, because you identify with Me, Jesus essentially says, persecution will come. You and I may not find ourselves flogged or arrested for our beliefs, but these words of Jesus have been comforting to countless numbers of His followers over the centuries. His warning has described the normal Christian experience for many generations and for many Christians today around the world

Jesus' words affirm that we may be people of faith, but we're not rubes. In fact, as I covered earlier, we're tapped into a wisdom and discernment that gives us great insight. And so we're sent into a threatening, even dangerous world, as Jesus acknowledges here, but we're sent with the power to be simultaneously shrewd and innocent. We're advised to keep our hearts clean even while we're getting our hands dirty in the mess of ministry. We can be in the world without being worldly. We can be good without being gullible, innocent but not ignorant. We're sent with a power that makes that possible, a power that conquers fear.

We're also sent with a strategy that embraces servanthood. Even amidst threat and misunderstanding, we serve others. That's what love does. As we just read from Mother Teresa: "Faith in action is love, and love in action is service." We put the needs of others—particularly their need for the Gospel of Jesus—before our own wants and needs. We are called to serve and be a blessing to this world. This is the essence of our mission and ministry and the definition of our Revolution. As Paul wrote to the Corinthians:

> So whether you eat or drink or whatever you do, do it all for the glory of God. Do not cause anyone to stumble, whether Jews, Greeks or the church of God—even as I try to please everyone in every way. For I am not seeking my own good but the good of many, so that they may be saved. (1 Corinthians 10:31-33)

So as we walk in this world, we have one aim in everything we do: decrease the distance between others and Jesus. We want our words and deeds to draw people closer to—and not farther from—Him in any and every way possible. Too often, we're better known for creating pre-requisites to faith in Jesus, religious hoops to jump through, behavioral qualifications to be met. Too often we get in the way of people getting on the Way. This should not be. Our mission, the reason we're sent, isn't to pursue our convenience or comfort—or even our conformity to a cultural religious ideal—but to seek the good of others "so that they may be saved." We serve this hurting and hungry world.

> **AS WE WALK IN THIS WORLD, WE HAVE ONE AIM IN EVERYTHING WE DO: DECREASE THE DISTANCE BETWEEN OTHERS AND JESUS.**

Such a mission is worthy of our highest effort and our deepest sacrifice. As Charles Spurgeon once energetically said:

> If sinners be damned, at least let them leap to hell over our dead bodies. And if they perish, let them perish with our arms wrapped

around their knees. If hell must be filled, let it be filled in the teeth of our exertions, and let no one go unwarned or unprayed for.[3]

We must be the people on the planet who care the most about the souls of others—all others, any others.

We are sent as Jesus was sent. Power from the Father is our engine. As Jesus prayed for His vulnerable disciples: "I will remain in the world no longer, but they are still in the world, and I am coming to you. Holy Father, protect them by the power of your name, the name you gave me..." (John 17:11) Service and sacrifice are our strategy, as they were His. As Jesus reminded His sometimes ambitious disciples: "The Son of Man did not come to be served, but to serve, and to give his life as a ransom for many." (Matthew 20:28)

WE ARE SENT WITH A MESSAGE. WE ARE TO BE HUMBLE AND CLEAR.

I'm always equal parts inspired and sobered by Paul's description of himself and his mission team in 2 Corinthians 5:20: "We are therefore Christ's ambassadors, as though God were making his appeal through us. We implore you on Christ's behalf: Be reconciled to God." I believe Paul's perspective as well as his message can be rightly taken up by all who call themselves disciples of Jesus.

An ambassador is defined as one sent by a sovereign as an authorized representative. To accept that we, like Paul, are just such authorized ambassadors of the King of Kings is to accept a weighty and adventurous responsibility. And accept it we should and must.

> **WE MUST BE THE PEOPLE ON THE PLANET WHO CARE THE MOST ABOUT THE SOULS OF OTHERS— ALL OTHERS, ANY OTHERS.**

Don't Jesus' departing words in Matthew 28:18-20 sound like the commissioning of such envoys? "All authority in heaven and on earth has been given to me." Jesus made it clear He is imminently and solely qualified to reign and exercise dominion. Such authority gives us confidence in our commission. "Therefore go and make disciples of all nations, baptizing them in the name of the Father and of the Son and of the Holy Spirit, and teaching them to obey everything I have commanded you." Here is the position description, the authorized responsibilities of His emissaries.

Ambassadors of Jesus, that's who we are, His regents sent to our regions of the world and, indeed, all regions of the world. We stand on earth on His behalf; we share His message and His love "as though God were making his appeal through us." That's heavy.

What is this message that changes the world? It's beautifully simple: "There is a God. He's for you, not against you. He loves you and wants very much to fill your life. He's made Himself real and known to us through Jesus Christ." And we make this earnest appeal: "Will you let Him be God? Please, turn to Him; He is ready to receive you. Jesus is the Way." Is there more to be included? Of course. There's the cross and repentance and forgiveness and grace and faith and baptism and so much more, but the pleading that pours from us is easily summarized in Paul's appeal: "Be reconciled to God."

> **WE STAND ON EARTH ON HIS BEHALF; WE SHARE HIS MESSAGE AND HIS LOVE "AS THOUGH GOD WERE MAKING HIS APPEAL THROUGH US." THAT'S HEAVY.**

This message calls for humility as well as clarity. That means we take the lead in loving people with whom we disagree—that's humility—while realizing we do no one any favors by watering down the truth—that's clarity.

Let's talk about loving people with whom we disagree, and remember: We can be right and still be very wrong. Sadly, Christians do this all the time. We can be doctrinally or biblically correct in our understanding of this or that issue, but if we don't lead with love—not just in our words but in our hearts—then we don't lead anyone anywhere worthwhile and we miss the point.

Let's say you have a friend or family member without Christ who's living in ways blatantly incongruent with Scripture. How do you treat them? For instance, do you have them—or their friends or significant others—over for holiday family celebrations? This is the kind of question I'm asked often as a pastor. Many who've approached me are concerned that if they do this they are implicitly extending their approval and acceptance of these sinful choices.

But let me assure you while I remind you: Everyone you're hosting makes immoral choices (including you and me), and we instinctively know our love for them and hospitality to them doesn't equal our endorsement of every choice they've made or are making. Stop and think: You and I have been carving that Thanksgiving turkey and gathering around that Christmas tree with a motley collection of flawed, confused, and downright sinful people. Just because some have been better at hiding it than others—or some of their sins have been easier for us to excuse or ignore—doesn't mean it's now time to turn off our love to those more forthright in their failing.

Here's the key: We must increase, not decrease the chances of an introduction between them and Jesus. Love, not rejection, does that. It's the Holy Spirit who does the changing in any of us as we turn to Jesus. We choose to love fallen people made in the image God. We see their preciousness, we see their potential. We're all about increasing the odds and expanding the opportunity of someone getting a realistic chance to say yes to Jesus and thus opening themselves to biblical truth and the Spirit's sanctifying work. Love is what paves that path. And nothing less than love. We get to show that. We've got to show that.

That's sharing the message with humility. Now let's talk about clarity.

Recent to the writing of this book, an interesting BuzzFeed video was making its way around social media. It's entitled, *I'm a Christian, But I'm Not*. It has spawned tons of shares, over 1.3 million views, even a trending hashtag. It features a handful of millennials first completing the phrase "I'm a Christian, but I'm not..." with such disparaging adjectives as "uneducated," "closed-minded," "judgmental" or "ignorant." Sadly, that probably needed to be said.

Then they move on to answer the question "What are you?" with professions such as "I'm gay." "I'm queer." "I'm not afraid to talk about sex." "I'm a feminist." "I *do* believe in science." "I love me some Beyonce." And "I love wine." I'm saddened that some of these were deemed necessary to say in order to reassure viewers someone could be a Christian but not anti-women or

> LOVE PAVES THE PATH. AND NOTHING LESS THAN LOVE. WE GET TO SHOW THAT. WE'VE GOT TO SHOW THAT.

anti-science. But what troubles me most is what's not said. People are free to love wine and Beyonce, but no one says, "I love Jesus." In fact, His name isn't mentioned at all.

This absence becomes especially pronounced and heartbreaking as they answer the final question: "What do you want people to know about Christianity?" The viewer is assured that "every Christian is different" and "we're not all kind of crazy" and that "at its core, it's really about love and acceptance and being a good neighbor." And to summarize, "I think everybody is on their own path to wherever they're trying to go. We're all people and love is the most important thing."[4]

Now, no one should be surprised that a BuzzFeed video isn't *The Didache*. I get that. These are the folks who bring us videos like "Gingers get spray tans for the first time" and "What bros do before a date" (and many entertaining, useful, and informative videos of all kinds.) But still... The entire revelation of Scripture and the insights of 2,000 years of Christian teaching get boiled down to that? That it's shallow and malinformed is a given; that such a view of our precious faith is permeating our culture is tragic. No Jesus, no cross, no real grace because there's no real sin, no real change, no empty tomb, and—did I mention?—no Jesus.

> **TRUE HEALING FOR ANY OF US ONLY BEGINS BY CONFRONTING THE FACTS, HOWEVER BRUTAL THEY MAY SOMETIMES BE.**

This video highlights what this world wants people to know about Christianity: we're not really different and we're all okay. But remember *The Didache*. There are two ways and they are very different, and we're not okay on just any one we choose or make up as we go, but only one. Only one.

And to say so is not condemning or judging. We can't send a mixed message. Remember what Jesus said in John 8:11 to the woman caught in adultery: "Neither do I condemn you." (That's grace.) "Go and sin no more." (That's truth.) But too many times in our society we instead hear the message, "Neither do I condemn you. Go and sin some more." And if we're not careful, we can do the same. In our sincere desire to not injure others (or come off as jerks) we spare them the pain of necessary truths and do them more harm than good. True healing for any of us only begins by confronting the facts, however brutal they may sometimes be. As Dallas Willard warns:

> The world can no longer be left to mere diplomats, politicians, and business leaders. They have done the best they could, no doubt. But this is an age for spiritual heroes—a time for men and women to be heroic in their faith and in spiritual character and power. The greatest danger to the Christian church today is that of pitching its message too low.[5]

The message of Jesus we share is about a free gift and a high calling, about grace bringing freedom *from* sin, not granting freedom *to* sin. God help us when we dilute it for easier consumption. And we must begin by not pitching the message too low to ourselves by being merely "Christians"—a term at best drained of its meaning and at worst twisted beyond recognition—but being disciples of Jesus, keepers of the Way.

James says that "whoever turns a sinner from the error of their way"—remember there are distinctly different "ways" and some are simply wrong, incorrect, in error—"will save them from death and cover over a multitude of sins." (James 5:20) Error and sin lead to death, but they can be "covered" and indeed have been by Jesus. This is the message the world most needs and the only one that can change it—one person, one heart at a time.

We are sent on a rescue mission with a message spoken loudly with actions and lovingly with words, shared both shrewdly and innocently, with both truth and grace.

And let's get super-clear on *why* we are sent: We're sent because someone's lost and Someone's looking.

That's right, our King is a father who relentlessly longs for reunion with His children. The message of the cross and the empty tomb is that He has gone to the greatest of lengths to make that reunion possible. Now He sends us to share that message with His lost children.

People are lost because they don't know better, lost because they're weak and worn by this world, and lost because they willfully put themselves in first place and ignore God. But no matter...God is looking, searching, and rescuing. To Him no one is a lost cause.

How does God search? How do lost people get found by Him? The answer is worth repeating. His mission is our mantra:

> Therefore go and make disciples of all nations, baptizing them in the name of the Father and of the Son and of the Holy Spirit, and teaching them to obey everything I have commanded you. And surely I am with you always, to the very end of the age. (Matthew 28-18-20)

Someone's lost and Someone's looking. Someone's missing and Someone's searching, therefore go. I actually believe we're going to held responsible for this. We find great comfort in Jesus' promise to be with us always. We should also find in those words great accountability. He's both empowering His Church and keeping an eye on us. As He should. His urgency must be ours as well. There is no keeping of His Way without keeping to His *why*. God forgive us when we forget this.

> GOD DID NOT SEND HIS SON INTO THE WORLD
> TO CONDEMN THE WORLD,
> BUT TO SAVE THE WORLD THROUGH HIM.
> [JOHN 3:17]

Many people get the impression—too often justifiably so—that Christians delight in condemning them. This is not only heartbreaking, it's counterproductive to Christ's mission. Remember: our *Resistance* is about our personal holiness and our *Rebellion* is about our own non-conformity to a secular culture, not about castigating others or pronouncing self-righteous judgments over them.

Jesus didn't hesitate to teach that life without Him is a sinking ship, but He always did so while throwing a life preserver. And He's our model. Think about how we change the world: Do I tend to think this Revolution is accomplished more by tearing down or by building up?

SHARING THE MESSAGE OF JESUS MEANS SHARING HOPE THAT WHO WE'VE BEEN NEED NOT DICTATE WHO WE'LL BE.

———— WE PRAY ————

"Jesus, You were sent to rescue me, not reject me. Thank You."

AS YOU SENT ME INTO THE WORLD, I HAVE SENT THEM INTO THE WORLD.
[JOHN 17:18]

Jesus makes a powerful statement in this prayer to the Father. Jesus says His disciples—including us, His disciples today—are sent *just as He was*. How was Jesus sent? He was sent full of both compassion and authority. He was sent to teach the truth to whomever would listen. He was sent to give away His life. He was sent *into the world*.

And now the way He is sent into the *whole world* is through us. We, His sent disciples, are His force multiplier. What a thrill. What a sense of adventure this truth conveys. Reflect and ask: Do I see myself as simply born here, just living here? Or can I see myself as *sent* here by God for a purpose?

> **WE ARE COMMISSIONED BY CHRIST TO INVADE EVERY CORNER OF THIS PLANET WITH HIS LOVE AND AMAZING GRACE.**

---WE PRAY---

"Father, thank You for sending Jesus. Jesus, thank You for sending me."

> I AM SENDING YOU OUT LIKE SHEEP AMONG WOLVES. THEREFORE BE AS SHREWD AS SNAKES AND AS INNOCENT AS DOVES.
> [MATTHEW 10:16]

Being sent by Jesus is not without its risks. And though we needn't be afraid, we're wise to recognize the world can be a threatening and dangerous place. It may seem to some that our emphasis on meekness, kindness, and holiness makes us resemble simple sheep, clueless to the ravenous forces that surround us. But that would misread the situation. The Holy Spirit in us gives us a sharp discernment that's not at all dulled by goodness.

Jesus advises us to maintain our high ethics without sacrificing our street smarts. We needn't be worldly to understand how the world works. We can be good without being gullible. Stop and think: How can I shrewdly make a strategic difference in this world?

> **INNOCENCE DOESN'T EQUAL IGNORANCE. FAITH DOESN'T MAKE US NAIVE. WE KNOW TOO WELL WHAT AILS THIS WORLD.**

WE PRAY

"My Shepherd, send me into this world with Your wisdom and grace."

I AM NOT SEEKING MY OWN GOOD BUT THE GOOD OF MANY, SO THAT THEY MAY BE SAVED.
[1 CORINTHIANS 10:33]

Our Revolution is fueled by selflessness. It is the epitome of our Christlikeness and non-conformity. Consistently putting others before ourselves is a radical way to live.

This doesn't mean we don't take care of ourselves or do nothing for ourselves. But it does mean recognizing the only real way to change the world is breaking the cycle of our "selfie" culture. Remember, humility isn't about thinking less of yourself, but it is definitely about thinking of yourself less. And it's an increasingly uncommon virtue.

Seize the opportunity: How can I bring someone significantly closer to the love of Jesus today by seeking their good and not my own?

> **IN OUR NEW PRIORITIES, OTHERS' NEED FOR CHRIST COMES BEFORE OUR NEED FOR CONVENIENCE OR COMFORT.**

WE PRAY

"God, I set aside my preferences for the higher purposes of Your mission."

> WE ARE THEREFORE CHRIST'S AMBASSADORS,
> AS THOUGH GOD WERE MAKING HIS APPEAL
> THROUGH US. WE IMPLORE YOU ON
> CHRIST'S BEHALF: BE RECONCILED TO GOD.
> [2 CORINTHIANS 5:20]

People are lost and they don't know it. They're missing a relationship with their Creator and Father, though they don't always realize what the ache in their soul means. They need—we all need—reconciliation with God. His heart breaks to see people living without Him. It should break our hearts too.

So we're driven to restore the connection, to invite others to get right with God through Jesus. We're the go-between, making the proper introductions, urging anyone who will listen: "Be reconciled to God." Ask yourself: How and to whom can God make His appeal through me today?

> **AS REPRESENTATIVES OF OUR KING, WE MUST BE COMPELLED BY HIS SAME COMPASSION AND LOVE.**

---WE PRAY---

"Christ, give me Your heart for this world. Send Your message through me."

Remember this: Whoever turns a sinner from the error of their way will save them from death and cover over a multitude of sins.
[JAMES 5:20]

Ours is, without a doubt, a rescue mission. This isn't about winning arguments, it's about winning souls. Winning them back from the enemy's clutches, saving them from eternity without God. Sin deceptively makes a dead-end alley look like Times Square. We get to show people the Way.

And the stakes cannot be overstated. In every person's life, the issue of Christian faith is not a matter of personal preference (which religion I like best) or family heritage (how I was raised) or cultural norms (the faith of those around me); it's a matter of life and death.

Carefully consider: How easily can I forget what's at stake in this Revolution? How can I better remember this reality?

> **THOSE WHO DON'T YET KNOW JESUS DON'T NEED US TO REFUTE OR REJECT THEM, BUT TO RESCUE THEM.**

---WE PRAY---

"Lord, use me as a signpost pointing all to Your good and wise Way."

ADVANCE THE REVOLUTION

12
Exclude No One

It is perhaps the Bible's most quoted verse, known by many with an otherwise scant familiarity with or exposure to Scripture. It is John 3:16, in which Jesus said, "For God so loved the world that he gave his one and only Son, that whoever believes in him shall not perish but have eternal life." This is part of a larger conversation He had with a curious religious teacher named Nicodemus. They are words of Jesus about Himself.

Nicodemus was getting a crash course in everything Jesus was about and God's plan for the world. And it's revolutionary.

Maybe not to us because we've become so familiar with these words. But they would have been a real mind-blower for Nicodemus. Why is that? Because of one word: *whoever*. That word, to the ears of Nicodemus, must have put him on his heels, made him lean back in his chair. "Whoever?! Say what?"

The point of *whoever* is this: Jesus has opened the Way to live with our Creator, and it is open to whomever, to anyone, who will follow Him on it. "Whoever believes in him" means God loves the whole world, that no one is excluded from His plan.

You are whoever. Regardless of your past, your mistakes, your heritage, your parents' beliefs regarding God and religion, regardless of the size of your paycheck, your special talents or maybe your perceived lack of special talents, whether you're married, single, divorced, self-sufficient or codependent, introvert or extravert, successful or struggling, you can, as Jesus put it, "believe in Him." *Whoever* has no stipulations or prerequisites, no qualifiers or fine print. Anyone can believe.

And check out this other nugget: Love is in the past tense. God has always loved the world, including you and me. Before we cared about God or would give Him the time of day, He loved us. He knows everything about us, has always known us, loves us and has always loved us. It's not, "Oh, I love you *now* that you've done this or arrived at that decision." He already loves us all. He *loved* so He *gave*. "When we were still powerless, Christ died for the ungodly. ...God demonstrates his own love for us in this: While we were still sinners, Christ died for us." (Romans 5:6-8)

What has become routine started out as revolutionary. It still is. **Everyone is loved by God and has the potential to follow Him. This is the heart of the Gospel and must be our heart too.** It may be a latent potential, an untapped potential. But releasing that potential in others to say yes to Jesus is exactly how we change the world. It begins with seeing others differently and helping them see themselves more accurately and more fully.

The Gospel is for everyone. And we are for everyone too.

We are to be the greatest proponents of people. They should sense that we as Christians are for them, for their good and their growth and health as human beings.

Vince Antonucci, a pastor and church planter in Los Vegas, writes in *God for the Rest of Us*, "The people you think are least deserving of God's love may well be the people who need God's love the most. This may be difficult for you. These are people you've always been against." Think of the "culture wars" of recent decades and all the angst that still surrounds changing and often degrading cultural norms. In these arenas we Christians have been too easily known for what we're against and have come off as harsh and hateful. Vince goes on:

> **EVERYONE IS LOVED BY GOD AND HAS THE POTENTIAL TO FOLLOW HIM. THIS HEART OF THE GOSPEL MUST BE OUR HEART TOO.**

Understand: It doesn't mean their sin is ok. But neither is yours. It doesn't mean they don't have things they really need to change. But so do you. But it *does* mean God is for them. And is for you. It means that *everyone* needs to experience God's unconditional and life-changing love.[1]

Catch that? *Everyone*. Everyone needs the love of God. Jesus died for everyone. There isn't a single human being Jesus did not have in mind when He gave His life on that cross.

Remember what we've heard Paul declare: "Christ's love compels us." Why? "Because we are convinced that one died for all." (2 Corinthians 5:14) We love all people because Christ died for all people. That love indeed compels us to see everyone anew. As Paul concluded: "So from now on we regard no one from a worldly point of view." (2 Corinthians 5:16)

A worldly point of view doesn't see the whole picture, the spiritual reality. And this is a real problem, especially when we fail to recognize the faith capabilities of others. It's one of the worse ways we can fail them. Instead of seeing others and focusing on their potential to say yes to Jesus, we figure their probability of saying no to Him. This is a tragic miscalculation. However, in this new POV we don't write people off and write them out of God's love story. Though sadly, we Christians aren't always known for this.

> **INSTEAD OF FOCUSING ON OTHERS' POTENTIAL TO SAY YES, WE FIGURE THEIR PROBABILITY OF SAYING NO TO JESUS.**

Anne Rice, one of today's most successful writers, first won fame with her *Vampire Chronicles* in the 1970s. About a decade ago, she spoke of "a new spiritual beginning" as she re-embraced the Christian faith of her childhood and began writing books of historical fiction about the life of Christ.[2]

But in 2010 she announced her decision to "quit being a Christian." She reaffirmed her commitment to Christ, but it was that term *Christian* and all the baggage it carries today that really started to hang her up. "Christians have lost credibility in America as people who know how to love," she lamented.[3] Granted, that is one person's opinion, but nonetheless it's a tragic one. And, let's face it, far from the only one like it. Too often, she is correct. Let's work to make it less and less so.

Now more than ever we need to heed Paul's advice to the Colossians: "Be wise in the way you act toward outsiders; make the most of every opportunity." (Colossians 4:5) It is not at all far-reaching to state—in the context of all of Scripture—that the wisest and most opportunistic way to act toward outsiders is to love them, to be thoughtful to someone who has not yet said yes to Jesus or who's been so burnt by the Church that they've left the Way. When we encounter such people, the first thing we should be seeing is an *opportunity to love someone*. Love is the only thing that will pave such difficult paths and penetrate hardened hearts.

> **THERE ISN'T ANYONE WHO COULDN'T USE SOME JESUS-LOVE IN THEIR LIFE.**

There isn't anyone who couldn't use some Jesus-love in their life, even if they don't realize it's Jesus-love coming out of us. So don't hold back that love and don't qualify it. If you're going to love only people who no longer need Jesus to make some changes in their heart and mind and life, good luck with that. It's not going to happen. We can be conservative in our values, but we'd better be liberal in our love. We must be for everyone, just as the Gospel is.

The Gospel tells the whole truth. And we are to be truth-tellers too.

Love always tells the truth, and the truth is always best spoken in love. People—all of us originally—are deceived and in the dark. This is humanity's reality. The world is heavily under the influence of the lies, half-truths, and distractions of, yes, the devil. Godless philosophies prevail in much of our culture today.

While the devil is not solely behind everything that's wrong with the world, we can be sure he's happy about it—and responsible for no small part of it, directly or indirectly. (Even if we simply trace our current mess back to our forebears' fall in the garden—which essentially plays itself out in every human life—Satan is right there.) It's a story that's everyone's story. And it always starts with lies that keep people in the dark.

As John the Apostle wrote, "The one who does what is sinful is of the devil, because the devil has been sinning from the beginning." Meaning when we sin we find ourselves in Satan's camp, under his influence, buying his lying. "The reason the Son of God appeared was to destroy the devil's work." (1 John 3:8) We live in a new era. The Son of God has arrived to overpower and obliterate evil. He includes us in that insurgency. It begins by telling the truth.

All around us people fall for half-truths and outright lies; they wander from one distraction to another. Days are strung together into years and by such deception they are kept away from the beautiful, simple truth of the Gospel. It was George Orwell who said, "During times of universal deceit, telling the truth becomes a revolutionary act."[4] He was right. And we are here to tell the Gospel truth, which Tim Keller describes this way: "The gospel is this: We are more sinful and flawed in ourselves than we ever dared believe, yet at the very same time we are more loved and accepted in Jesus Christ than we ever dared hope."[5] That's a beautiful truth beautifully said. It's one we really shouldn't keep to ourselves.

> **THE SON OF GOD HAS ARRIVED TO OVERPOWER AND OBLITERATE EVIL. HE INCLUDES US IN THAT INSURGENCY. IT BEGINS BY TELLING THE TRUTH.**

Here's a sneaky way we sometimes trick ourselves into doing just that: We begin to think of our faith as a purely personal thing. It can sound serious and sober to say to ourselves and perhaps even to others, "My faith is a private matter, just between me and God." In this platitude we find a safe place to pocket our faith so we're not associated with bullhorns on sidewalks or socially awkward doorknockers or whatever and whoever else.

The problem with such an approach is that it also doesn't associate us with Jesus, and it's a misread of what Christian faith is all about. Maybe we're somewhat afraid of the opinions or even opposition of others, but Jesus said,

> Do not be afraid of them, for there is nothing concealed that will not be disclosed, or hidden that will not be made known. What I tell you in the dark, speak in the daylight; what is whispered in your ear, proclaim from the roofs. (Matthew 10:26-27)

Yes, faith—the impact of God's love and truth on our hearts—is an intensely personal thing. But that's where it starts, not where it stops. Jesus' words here remind us that what we sense from Him in the depth of our hearts and in the quietness of our minds is to be brought out where everyone can hear it and no one can miss it.

One great way we all can accomplish this is to simply be ourselves—our truest, brightest, redeemed selves—wherever we go and with whomever we are. When you and I are the same honest and unafraid Christian with everyone everywhere, we don't leave anyone out. And this is important at the very least because you and I have people in our lives—souls God has placed in our circle of care and influence—who deserve to hear the truth from someone they know and trust. "Why didn't you tell me? Why did you keep such a powerful thing private?" These are words we don't want to hear.

Realize this: We, as Christians who have come to understand the reality of life described by Scripture, grasp that sin (our own human selfishness and defiance of God) can kill us. Sin is killing everyone we know apart from Christ. When people walk away from God in little and large ways they are distancing themselves from life, the Giver of Life. Our bodies, as they are, one day give out, but our souls last forever. And sin kills our souls like a cancer. And so to keep the grace and love of Jesus private is as unthinkable to the scripturally-minded Christian as someone discovering the cure to cancer and keeping it to themselves. Who would do such a thing?

> **WHEN WE'RE THE SAME HONEST AND UNAFRAID CHRISTIAN WITH EVERYONE EVERYWHERE, THEN WE DON'T LEAVE ANYONE OUT.**

The Gospel both unifies and divides. And we are to keep post at the borderlands.

We have to recognize a painful but persistent reality. We stand at the borderlines of faith, at the fork in the road, always inviting others onto the Way of Jesus. But those borderlines can become battlelines. We know it. It's not easy. People do indeed choose sides. They may reject Jesus, and when they do it can feel like they reject us as well. And sometimes we are, in fact, rejected.

Exclude No One

Jesus warns that His Gospel draws lines of demarcation between its proponents and opponents, lines that sometimes run right through homes.

> Do not suppose that I have come to bring peace to the earth. I did not come to bring peace, but a sword. For I have come to turn
> > "a man against his father,
> >> a daughter against her mother,
> >
> > a daughter-in-law against her mother-in-law—
> >> a man's enemies will be the members of his own household." (Matthew 10:34-36)

This is what Gospel truth does. It's not up for interpretation. Jesus on that cross, Jesus leaving that tomb: It's a claim at which no one can merely shrug. It either draws you by its graceful beauty or offends you with its righteous simplicity. Christianity is not a dull or tame thing. It's a sword's edge. It's a wildfire. As Jesus put it elsewhere: "I have come to bring fire on the earth, and how I wish it were already kindled!" (Luke 12:49)

I'd like to tell you just a bit of the story of a nun known as Mother Maria of Paris. She became a nun in the 1920s and was almost immediately bothered by the business-as-usual air of the monasteries she visited. She expressed her angst with these words: "No one is aware that the world is on fire."

> **CHRISTIANITY IS NOT A DULL OR TAME THING. IT'S A SWORD'S EDGE. IT'S A WILDFIRE.**

Her energy and passion, as well as her disgust for what she perceived as a Church that had become ossified by traditionalism and had abandoned its ministry to the world, at times put her at odds with her superiors. "I could never be a good nun," she said at one point to her spiritual mentor. He answered, "I know. But I would like you to be a revolutionary nun." He unleashed her to be herself, the person God made her to be.

Thus began a life of opening homes as havens for the destitute and struggling. She lived among tramps and outcasts to show them the love of Christ. During World War II, Mother Maria began hiding Jews and helping transport them to safety out of France. She stood up to Nazis, sometimes in personal altercations. She paid for it with her life as she was shipped off to the Ravensbruck concentration camp, sent to a gas chamber just five weeks before the war's end.

I share her story not only because her actions are inspiring, but because of the spirit from which such courage and compassion was birthed. In these words of Mother Maria, hear her heart:

> Only once a person perceives the image of God in his brother will yet another mystery be revealed to him, which demands of him his most strenuous struggle. ...He will see how this image of God is obscured, distorted by an evil power. ...And in the name of the image of God, darkened by the devil, in the name of love for this image of God that pierces his heart, he will want to begin a struggle with the devil, to become an instrument of God in this terrible and scorching work.[6]

> **THIS IS WHERE A LIFE LIVED FOR OTHERS BEGINS: RECOGNIZING THEIR MARRED, MUTED DIVINITY AND DEDICATING OURSELVES TO CALLING IT OUT IN JESUS' NAME.**

This is where a life lived for others begins: recognizing the marred and muted divinity in those around us and dedicating ourselves to calling out their potential in Jesus' name. It's "scorching work," full of all the heat and friction found in rescuing prisoners from an enemy's camp. We do such work with pierced hearts and through "strenuous struggle." It's worth it. What we see in others can save their lives—and then who knows?—perhaps the lives of countless others. This is our post, if we will keep to it.

When it comes to saying yes to Jesus, we know not everyone *will*, but we mustn't forget anyone *can*. Consider the story of Norma McCorvey. Norma was Jane Roe in the Supreme Court case *Roe v. Wade* that legalized abortion.

In 1995, a pro-life group moved their national headquarters next to a clinic in Dallas, Texas that provided abortions. This clinic was managed by Norma McCorvey. The situation looked like a perfect storm for conflict, but instead became a perfect opportunity for conversation.

The pastor leading the pro-life group next door would join Norma when she'd step outside the back of the building for a smoke-break. They would talk. Eventually, Norma became convinced the Way of Jesus was the way she wanted to live.

What made the difference? Norma says it was the way Pastor Flip was simply real with her. One of the tipping point moments was when she realized the pastor liked the Beach Boys and had even been to a concert. She expressed her surprise that he was a normal guy. He answered, "I'm just a great big sinner saved by a great big God." She remembers:

> Of all the things I expected Flip to say, this wasn't one of them. ...I was shaken. What if the same things that happened to Flip happened to me? Nah. Couldn't happen. Not to Norma McCorvey. Not to Jane Roe. God wouldn't have her.[7]

We know better, and she learned better too. Norma came to understand that God so loved her that He gave His one and only Son, and that *whoever* believes in him shall not perish but have eternal life. After her conversion, Norma McCorvey dedicated herself to pro-life work, starting her own ministry, "Roe No More," and in 2003 she went to court in an attempt to overturn *Roe v. Wade*. All because someone refused to write her off or write her out of God's love story.

So from now on we regard no one from a worldly point of view.
[2 Corinthians 5:16]

If our Revolution is one of selfless love and humility, it will change the way we see others. Not only does the Holy Spirit make us more patient and less easily angered, we are also made more hopeful about people. We begin to see that, no matter what, through Christ people are loaded with godly possibilities.

We mustn't underestimate the value of any and every human soul. In a sense, while Jesus was nailed to the cross He saw every one of us and estimated we were worth it. If the value of humanity is based on the price Jesus was willing to pay, then we are all precious beyond imagination. Take a look around: Who in my life have I ignored or neglected, but about whom Jesus says, "Worth it."?

> **NO ONE'S IRREDEEMABLE. EVERYONE'S DRIPPING WITH POTENTIAL. EACH PERSON IS RELENTLESSLY LOVED BY GOD.**

---WE PRAY---

"Father, give me Your eyes to see others as You see them."

BE WISE IN THE WAY YOU ACT TOWARD OUTSIDERS; MAKE THE MOST OF EVERY OPPORTUNITY.
[COLOSSIANS 4:5]

Let's face it: Christians have a rough reputation when it comes to how we treat those who aren't yet Christians. And sadly, the worse some self-described believers behave the more headlines it makes. So we who strive to hold to the truth while treating everyone with love and respect have our work cut out for us. But this is indeed our work, and it's essential we do it wisely.

It's an often repeated but nonetheless profound observation: You are the first Bible some people read. So we must be thoughtful in our relationships with anyone who hasn't yet said yes to Jesus...and not be a reason they keep saying no. Ask yourself: When it comes to others coming to Jesus, am I more often an obstacle or an opportunity?

> **THOSE WHO DON'T YET KNOW JESUS NEED US TO BE CAREFUL AND PERSISTENT IN OUR LOVE FOR THEM.**

WE PRAY

"Lord, let me never be a hurdle between others and their path to You."

> DO NOT BE AFRAID OF THEM, FOR THERE IS NOTHING CONCEALED THAT WILL NOT BE DISCLOSED, OR HIDDEN THAT WILL NOT BE MADE KNOWN. WHAT I TELL YOU IN THE DARK, SPEAK IN THE DAYLIGHT; WHAT IS WHISPERED IN YOUR EAR, PROCLAIM FROM THE ROOFS.
> [MATTHEW 10:26-27]

In the passage above, Jesus is preparing His disciples for the opposition they will inevitably face. He's instilling in them (and us) confidence and instructing them (and us) to not fear. Why? Because we, His followers, are indeed—despite what pundits may say—on the right side of history. The truth will come out in the end. We need not—and must not—hold back.

It's comfortable—and, if we're honest, convenient—to think of our faith as a completely private thing, just between us and God. But that's not what Jesus has in mind; that's not how He changes the world. Consider: What am I afraid of when it comes to going public with my faith?

> **A DAY WILL COME WHEN THOSE WHO ATTACK GOD'S PEOPLE DISCOVER WHOM THEY WERE TRULY OPPOSING.**

---WE PRAY---

"Lord God, You know all things. May my only fear be displeasing You."

THE REASON THE SON OF GOD APPEARED WAS TO DESTROY THE DEVIL'S WORK.
[1 JOHN 3:8]

While the devil is not solely behind everything that's wrong with the world, we can be sure he's happy about it...and responsible for no small part of it, directly or indirectly. He has a long career of bringing pain, inciting hate, and fostering separation between people and their Creator. This is his work. And he loves his job.

As followers of Jesus, our work is to put Satan out of business, to overthrow his tables of exchange and drive out his seats of influence from the temples of human hearts. We are to do all we can to end evil, injustice, and oppression wherever we find it. Consider: Instead of simply being *against* something wrong, how can I *actually stop* it?

> **SATAN HAS BEEN BUSY SINCE THE FALL OF HUMANKIND. THROUGH JESUS WE CAN HAND HIM HIS PINK SLIP.**

---WE PRAY---

"Son of God, Your entrance into this world and my heart trumps every evil."

I HAVE COME TO BRING FIRE ON THE EARTH, AND HOW I WISH IT WERE ALREADY KINDLED!
[LUKE 12:49]

Throughout Scripture, fire is a powerful analogy of God and His work...and for good reason. Fire refines gold by burning off the dross, just as God refines our character. As fire brings warmth, God brings passion to our hearts. As fire brings light, God brings wisdom to our minds. Fire spreads. Fire consumes completely. So does God and His love.

Jesus came to set the whole world on fire so that all could be warmed by the heat of His Spirit and guided by the light of His truth. That starts with His fire in us. Christianity is not a tame thing. It's a wildfire. Ask yourself: How flammable am I?

> **JESUS IGNITES IN US A ZEAL TO FOLLOW HIM, A FERVOR TO LOVE OTHERS, AND A PASSION TO CHANGE THE WORLD.**

---WE PRAY---

"Jesus, set me aflame for You and let the world watch me burn."

Do not suppose that I have come to bring peace to the earth. I did not come to bring peace, but a sword.
[Matthew 10:34]

In this passage, Jesus warns that His Gospel draws lines of demarcation between its proponents and opponents; lines that sometimes run right through homes. At the same time that we are being united with our Heavenly Father and the family of God, all other relationships are being redefined, our loyalties and closest ties realigned.

This doesn't mean we don't strive to love and respect everyone, but Jesus is preparing us for the reality of the situation. Truth is not up for interpretation. It can divide as well as unite. Remember: In many ways we're outlaws on the outskirts. Think about it: Am I ready to be rejected because of my involvement in Christ's Revolution?

> **IT IS A PAINFUL BUT PERSISTENT REALITY THAT DEVOTION TO JESUS CAN DIVIDE US FROM OTHERS.**

---WE PRAY---

"Jesus, let me not be lulled into a false sense of security."

13
GO AHEAD

In a letter historians call *The Epistle to Diognetus*, an unknown second century disciple wrote to a skeptic named Diognetus to answer his questions about the strange new religion called Christianity. The opening lines of his letter capture what people must have found so appealing about followers of Jesus roughly 17 and a half centuries ago.

> I have noticed, my lord Diognetus, the deep interest you have been showing in Christianity, and the close and careful inquiries you have been making about it. You would like to know what God Christians believe in, and what sort of cult they practice which enables them to set so little store by this world, and even to make light of death... You are curious, too, about the warm fraternal affection they all feel for one another. You wonder, too, why this new race or way of life has appeared on earth now and not earlier.[1]

This was a time of intense persecution for Christians. How they lived and how they died was noteworthy. There was something so different and compelling, so curious and attractive about these Christians, these people of the Way.

And let's notice that phrase, "even to make light of death." Such an observation would not be made casually. A reputation deserving that description is earned in blood. It doesn't happen by accident, but is the mark of people whose priorities are realigned and whose vision of life, the world, and what it all means is redefined...people who keep to the Way no matter what.

This reminds me of a young world-changer named David in the Old Testament. The people of God, including his own older brothers, were frozen in fear as they faced a people and a culture that wanted to wipe them out. No one would go and face this antagonist. Their faith was drained of courage. David looked around at the inaction and apathy of God's people and couldn't believe what he was seeing. He asked incredulously, "Is there not a cause?" (1 Samuel 17:29 KJV) Then, to the confoundment of all, he did what needed to be done and no one else would do.

We too may be tempted to be negligent, hesitant, and afraid. But we must be faithful, bold, and fearless. **This revolution of Jesus begins with our personal turnaround and leads to his global takeover.** Changed people change the world.

OUR DEVOTION TO JESUS IS A SUBVERSIVE ACT. LET'S BE FAITHFUL.

We can be tempted to believe that our negligence of Jesus and His Way, His cause, is only of consequence to us, and conversely that our faithfulness to Jesus is of benefit mostly to us. As if our devotion to Jesus is sort of like eating right or exercising—good for us if we choose to do so, but otherwise no big deal. "I make it to church when I can and engage with some Scripture when I'm feeling it, but in the end it's all good." But perhaps there's more going on.

The Apostle John describes the real conflict that's happening within and around us as a contest between two spirits, two spiritual perspectives or approaches: one that acknowledges the reality of Jesus and one that doesn't. This second one he calls "the spirit of the antichrist," which stands—as the word implies—against Jesus. Such a spirit was embodied in the opponents of Christianity and false teachers of John's day as well as in the fear, falsehood, and selfishness that besets every believer's soul.

> **THE REVOLUTION OF JESUS BEGINS WITH OUR PERSONAL TURNAROUND AND LEADS TO HIS GLOBAL TAKEOVER.**

This is the spirit of the antichrist, which you have heard is coming and even now is already in the world. You, dear children, are from God and have overcome them, because the one who is in you is greater than the one who is in the world. (1 John 4:3-4)

He wants these Christians to know that what they have going on in themselves as people who have faith in Jesus is no inconsequential thing. It is larger and more powerful and more impactful in changing this world than any other "spirit" that exists. Don't underestimate it.

See, when we individually let up off the gas of our own faith we are also decreasing the overall power, effectiveness, impact of the cause. The spirit in this world wants to deny Jesus and silence His followers. And when you and I slip into seeing our Christianity as a nice upgrade to our life and not the world-changing force it is, we go dormant and get quiet, the world remains unaffected, and in a very real sense the spirit of the antichrist has done its work.

John knew what this spirit of the antichrist looked and sounded like. Decades before writing his letter, John and Peter prayed for a sick man (see Acts chapter four). That man was healed and many, many people came to faith in Jesus. This gets them in hot water with the Jewish religious leaders, who ask them, "By what power or what name did you do this?" Then Peter, filled with the Holy Spirit, said to them, "It is by the name of Jesus Christ of Nazareth, whom you crucified but whom God raised from the dead, that this man stands before you healed." This comes straight from Jesus, Peter said. He did just this kind of thing when He was with us, and He's still doing it because *He's still with us.*

> **WHEN WE LET UP OFF THE GAS OF OUR OWN FAITH, WE ARE ALSO DECREASING THE OVERALL IMPACT OF THE CAUSE.**

(You might think, "Well, that's great and that's in the Bible, but I've never prayed for anyone and seen them healed." I would say you haven't *yet*, but don't rule it out. I've seen that happen for sure, in miraculous ways. Not often, but often enough. Perhaps that's true of you as well. So keep praying, keep believing. Faithfulness to Christ is radical and world-changing.)

The larger point is that changed lives are the greatest miracles, the greatest healing. A life turned around and lived for Jesus is the weightiest, most beautiful evidence of God's reality. The healing Jesus brings to a life—psychologically, emotionally, mentally, spiritually, and yes, physically, is real and powerful. This world needs it desperately and you and I do too. We can receive it and share it in the name of Jesus Christ of Nazareth, crucified and raised from the dead. It is in that Name we stand and do anything good.

> **THE POWER OF OUR FAITH IS DIRECTLY CORRELATED TO OUR PROXIMITY TO JESUS.**

Peter continues, "Salvation is found in no one else, for there is no other name under heaven given to mankind by which we must be saved."

There it is. Drop the mic.

This took guts. This was sheer faith at full blast. "When they saw the courage of Peter and John and realized that they were unschooled, ordinary men, they were astonished and they took note that these men had been with Jesus." The power of our faith is directly correlated to our proximity to Jesus.

Friend, be *with* Jesus. Don't leave Him. Keep believing Him. You will become so much more than you ever realized you could be simply by being and staying *with Him*.

And He's with you. There's power in your corner. Be faithful. It's a subversive act. It's an insurgency of righteousness. It's a mutiny against mediocrity. It's the truest paradigm shift there is. It's an upheaval of the status quo of pain and grief. It's an uprising of healing and hope. "Who is it that overcomes the world?" John later asks. His answer is profound and unchanged since that day standing next to Peter: "Only the one who believes that Jesus is the Son of God." (1 John 5:5)

THIS WORLD IS IN DESPERATE NEED. GO BE BOLD.

We may tend to be hesitant and hold back. That's usually because our desire for security outweighs our sense of urgency, our need for comfort drowns out our sense of calling. But we can dare to be more. Hear these words from the great preacher and author, A.B. Simpson: "God is preparing His heroes. And when the opportunity comes, He can fit them into their places in a moment, and the world will wonder where they came from."[2] I love that. Like Peter and John, the Holy Spirit is with us to give us words to say and things to do at the right time and in the right way.

Let's keep looking at Acts chapter four.

"What are we going to do with these men?" the religious leaders asked. This is the question that won't go unasked and can't go unanswered, not then and not now. Ultimately, the one thing Jesus-followers cannot be is ignored. Not really, not for long. Our message must be dealt with and responded to one way or another. Here's their conclusion:

> Everyone living in Jerusalem knows they have performed a notable sign, and we cannot deny it. But to stop this thing from spreading any further among the people, we must warn them to speak no longer to anyone in this name. (Acts 4:16-17)

Tell me that doesn't feel familiar, that this isn't starting to sound less and less like a sentiment from 20 centuries ago and more like a voice in our ears today.

"Stop spreading this any further. Speak no longer. Keep it to yourself."

So the leaders followed through and "commanded them not to speak or teach at all in the name of Jesus." But Peter and John replied, "Which is right in God's eyes: to listen to you, or to him? You be the judges! As for us, we cannot help speaking about what we have seen and heard." It was clear to them what they would do and keep doing. Essentially they said, "We'll keep spreading the good news of Jesus; we can't help it! It's the right thing to do."

> **THE HOLY SPIRIT IS WITH US TO GIVE US WORDS TO SAY AND THINGS TO DO AT THE RIGHT TIME AND IN THE RIGHT WAY.**

"Which is right in God's eyes?" they ask with clarifying conviction. This is far from an inconsequential question, a simple matter of personal spiritual devotion or individual preference. How you and I answer that question is pivotal not just for us but for this world. God is real and has a real mastery of what is right. We learn what is right from Him. Understanding what is right and doing it, and helping others see what is right in God's eyes and doing it, is how we change the world.

Let me provide an example of what I mean. *The New York Times* recently ran an article entitled, "ISIS Enshrines a Theology of Rape." It is a tragic and terrible example of getting what we're talking about so very wrong.

The lead paragraph tells the story of an Islamic State fighter taking the time to explain to a 12-year-old girl that what he was about to do was not a sin but instead approved by his god. He bound her hands and gagged her. Then he knelt to pray before and after he raped her.

The article goes on to provide a thorough analysis of the use of sex slavery by the Islamic State, including the systematic rape of women and girls. One 15-year-old testified, "He said that raping me is his prayer to God."[3]

You can't tell me we're not engaged in a war of ideas, of thinking, yes, even of theology. Because what each of us believes to be right in the eyes of God will lead us to either beautiful or terrible places. Light or dark, truth or lies. The tears of heaven or the satisfied smirk of hell itself on earth. Hear these words of Jesus now like you've never heard them before...

> Therefore go and make disciples of all nations, baptizing them in the name of the Father and of the Son and of the Holy Spirit, and *teaching them to obey everything I have commanded you*. And surely I am with you always, to the very end of the age. (Matthew 28:19-20)

On these words we have staked everything and to these ends we dedicate ourselves as Jesus-followers: All authority is His; we will spread His love and message; He will be with us always. We will teach with our words and our actions—and with the sacrifice of our lives, if necessary—the beauty of obeying Jesus, the wonder of His Way. Inaction is not an option. Apathy is pathetic.

Dr. King's words in his *Letter from a Birmingham Jail* speak to us today: "We will have to repent in this generation not merely for the vitriolic words and actions of the bad people, but for the appalling silence of the good people."[4] Let us not be among the silent, so-called good people. These are times of courage, of testing, of rising to the challenge before us. Let's be bold.

GOD WANTS TO USE US TO TAKE OVER THE WORLD. LET'S GO BE FEARLESS.

This isn't a phase I use lightly or an idea I ever want to make sound trite. God's goal of taking over (really, re-taking) the world with His love and grace through His new and global family is absolutely what the mission of Jesus is all about. One heart, one person, one courageous action, one compassionate word at a time. Dallas Willard frames it this way:

> In sending out his disciples, Jesus set in motion a *perpetual world revolution*, one that is still in process and will continue until God's will is done on earth as it is in heaven. As this revolution culminates, all the forces of evil known to humankind will be defeated, and the goodness of God will be known, accepted, and joyously conformed to in every aspect of human life.[5]

This isn't for someone else or for some future day. This call to courage isn't issued only to the most qualified among us or the most persecuted in a faraway nation. It's for every Christian. We're keeping to a Way that has not changed. We live where we live and when we live, but *how* will we live? How will we live out this call? Will we leverage our life for all it's worth to make a difference in our corner of the world? The cause in front of us is clear.

To be sure, the Revolution will look different through each of us. What you say and do, how you're bold and how you're fearless will not be the same as someone else's boldness and fearlessness. The difference you're going to make in this world will be uniquely yours. Lean into it. Love your enemy, feed the hungry, look after the needy, visit the lonely, teach the confused, tell the story, turn the tide. Be. Not. Afraid. How else is it going to happen, without the Church being what it's meant to be, without you and I being what we're meant to be? A world-changing force.

> **THE DIFFERENCE YOU'RE GOING TO MAKE IN THE WORLD WILL BE UNIQUELY YOURS. LEAN INTO IT.**

On a most troubling evening just hours before He went to the cross, Jesus assured His disciples, "Peace I leave with you; my peace I give you. I do not give to you as the world gives. Do not let your hearts be troubled and do not be afraid." (John 14:27) We live in troubled times full of headlines that trouble us; fear finds multiple potential points of entry into our hearts. But Jesus says we mustn't *let* our hearts be troubled, mustn't allow fear to win the day. We get to choose to not let fear in and not let fear win.

In Acts chapter four the disciples were simply warned. But, of course, they wouldn't—really couldn't—stop. So in chapter five they are beaten.

> They called the apostles in and had them flogged. Then they ordered them not to speak in the name of Jesus, and let them go. The apostles left the Sanhedrin, rejoicing because they had been counted worthy of suffering disgrace for the Name. (Acts 5:40-41)

This is the spirit of a revolutionary: to count it a blessing to suffer, to "make light even of death" as the early believers were described in *The Epistle to Diognetus*. To see ourselves spent, not on pursuing our own comforts and achievements, but spent and poured out for the cause. I fear it's a blessing we don't know enough of. Os Guinness has stated the situation clearly:

> **CAN WE SAY, "THIS TRIAL EXISTS IN MY LIFE BECAUSE I AM A FOLLOWER OF THE WAY. ISN'T THAT AWESOME?"**

> To be sure, faithfulness is costly in the short term. It is upstream and against the flow, and the flow that was once politically correct can suddenly become a raging and life-threatening intolerance. But costly though that stand may be, it is never as costly as the long-term price of rejecting the authority of Jesus and abandoning the way of life in the gospel.[6]

We may not find ourselves flogged, but will we let ourselves get fatigued? We may not be put on trial, but can we endure some trying circumstances? Can we experience some inconvenience for Jesus? Sacrifice some comfort, give until it hurts, stay up late or get up early? Do whatever it is the Lord has put in front of us to do for the Name? And then rejoice that whatever we've endured was because we enjoy the privilege of belonging to Jesus? Can we say, "This trial exists in my life because I am a follower of the Way. Isn't that awesome?" God give us just such a spirit of perseverance, joy, and courage.

In Acts 5:42 we read: "Day after day"—consistently because it was simply who they were—"in the temple courts and from house to house"—wherever they went because everyone needs to hear—"they never stopped teaching and proclaiming the good news that Jesus is the Messiah"—because the mission is to take over the world one redeemed heart at a time. Nothing to fear, eternity to gain.

How does this happen? We heard it from that second century voice at the beginning of this chapter. Death doesn't mean what it used to. It's a recurring paradox throughout the New Testament: We are fully alive and as good as dead. "I have been crucified with Christ and I no longer live," Paul wrote to the Galatians, "but Christ lives in me." (2:20) And in his second letter to the Corinthians he observed, "We who are alive are always being given over to death for Jesus' sake, so that his life may be revealed in our mortal body." (4:11) Most boldly he declared to the Philippians, "For to me, to live is Christ and to die is gain." (1:21)

Remember that mid-third century plague and the Christians the bishop Dionysius wrote about: "Heedless of danger, they took charge of the sick...and with them departed this life serenely happy. ...Many, in nursing and curing others, transferred their death to themselves and died in their stead." Plagues come in many forms and sweep away lives in many ways. Who will go and run to the pain, take charge of the sick, heed not danger, and minister in the name of Christ? Those men and women who keep the Way will. We will go.

"Go," that tightly-packed initial verb of the Great Commission, is not it's primary one. *Mathēteuō*, which we translate "make disciples," is the center of the command, the only imperative verb in the sentence. In other words, the first only matters if the second gets done. And taken together, they forge the engine of our Revolution: "In your (plural) going"—more precisely translated—"develop students/disciples" of Jesus. It's our manifesto, our marching orders, our mandate. *Going* is our default setting. *Forming disciples* is our core mission.

Such formation can only begin when current disciples faithfully, boldly, and fearlessly answer the call of the cause and tell people about Jesus. So let's faithfully follow Him, staying near Him, learning from Him. Let's boldly use our words—even and especially the Name of Jesus—to build bridges between people and their Father. Let's fearlessly demonstrate that death is no longer a threat to us, and that what others see as risk we take as responsibility.

"How can they believe in him if they have never heard about him? And how can they hear about him unless someone tells them? And how will anyone go and tell them without being sent?" (Romans 10:14-15 NLT) We *will* go; we *are* sent. Sent with a love that's practical, powerful, and relentless. Sent with a diversity of creativity that can actually improve this world in measurable ways. Sent with a courage to set things right and do what's right no matter what. Sent to make disciples. It's time to go.

So go ahead and believe in Jesus, and believe Jesus when He says He's always with us.

Go ahead and love the people of this world. There is no fear in love. Our culture is changing, but there's nothing to be afraid of.

Go ahead and embrace everyone. It doesn't mean you're embracing everything they do. It never has meant that. We can be limitless in love and not give an inch on truth. Go ahead and try it.

Go ahead and run to the pain and mess of ministry. The worst situations—the thorniest problems, the gravest injustices—are by definition the most difficult and demanding. And the best work of all.

Is there not a cause? There is. And it's worth it.

THE ONE WHO IS IN YOU IS GREATER THAN THE ONE WHO IS IN THE WORLD.
[1 JOHN 4:4]

We Christians may not always seem like much, either to ourselves or to the world. But there's more to us than meets the eye. We have the capacity to resist our lower natures, rebel against conventional wisdom, and revolutionize unjust systems. Throughout history, Christians have taken the lead in founding hospitals, opening orphanages, abolishing slavery, protecting children, empowering women, and educating the poor.

For all this world's bluster and bragging, it's no match for Christ's Spirit within us. The Good News of Jesus is not unopposed, but it is unstoppable...in us and in this world. Consider yourself: Do I believe I carry within myself the power to put hell on notice and change this world?

> **AS POWERFUL OR PERSUASIVE AS THIS WORLD'S SYSTEM MAY APPEAR, IT IS NO MATCH FOR THE SPIRIT WHO FILLS US.**

---WE PRAY---

"Holy Spirit, give me godly confidence of Your greatness within me."

WHO IS IT THAT OVERCOMES THE WORLD? ONLY THE ONE WHO BELIEVES THAT JESUS IS THE SON OF GOD.
[1 JOHN 5:5]

We must not let our faith, however familiar or historic, become drained of its potent meaning. Christianity is revolutionary. No other religion dares to make the audacious claims ours makes: God incarnate voluntarily died and then walked out of the grave, ascended to heaven and promised to return, while in the meantime indwelling each of His followers with His dynamic spiritual presence. These beliefs are bold and without equal.

Believing these things can't help but change us. It brings a "new normal" to our lives, which we bring wherever we go. The influence and importance of this world and its ways helplessly fade when compared with the raw energy and beauty of the Gospel. Look within: How has my belief in who Jesus is helped me—and how can it help me— overcome the world?

> **GENUINELY, SIMPLY PUTTING OUR FAITH IN JESUS IS A SUBVERSIVE ACT. CHANGED PEOPLE CHANGE THE WORLD.**

---WE PRAY---

"Jesus, Son of God, I believe You and I believe in Your cause to rule the world."

> PEACE I LEAVE WITH YOU; MY PEACE I GIVE YOU.
> I DO NOT GIVE TO YOU AS THE WORLD GIVES.
> DO NOT LET YOUR HEARTS BE TROUBLED
> AND DO NOT BE AFRAID.
> [JOHN 14:27]

A little later in this same discourse with His disciples, Jesus said, "In this world you will have trouble. But take heart! I have overcome the world." Jesus helps us confront the brutal facts. This world is a troubled and troubling place. While we're in it, we need Him in us.

The world gives a counterfeit peace based on things going our way, people liking us, and our wants being satisfied. This is a mirage. Jesus grants genuine peace based not on freedom from conflict but on restful confidence in Him as we work through conflict. This is the irony of our calling: we are peaceful disturbers of the peace, simultaneously disruptive and constructive. Ask yourself: To what or whom have I assigned the power to rob me of my peace?

> **WHAT WE NEED MOST IN OUR DEPTHS WILL NEVER BE SUPPLIED IN THIS UNSTABLE AND UNRELIABLE WORLD.**

---WE PRAY---

"Jesus, let my peace come from confidence in You, not calm circumstances."

GO AND MAKE DISCIPLES OF ALL NATIONS, BAPTIZING THEM IN THE NAME OF THE FATHER AND OF THE SON AND OF THE HOLY SPIRIT, AND TEACHING THEM TO OBEY EVERYTHING I HAVE COMMANDED YOU. AND SURELY I AM WITH YOU ALWAYS, TO THE VERY END OF THE AGE.
[MATTHEW 28:19-20]

Here they are in black and white: the last standing orders of our commanding officer. Read and hear those verbs: *go* and *make* and *baptize* and *teach* and *obey*. Nothing inactive or inconsequential here. Nothing ambiguous either. Jesus could not have been more clear: Get going…there's work to do.

And He promises something very profound: in our going He'll always be going with us. Perhaps familiarity has lessened for us the impact of that pledge. Even as He was *leaving Earth*, He was not *leaving us*. Would not leave us. Would never leave us. No matter how far the mission takes us. Pause and reflect: Jesus said He'd stay with me, but He also commanded me to go. Am I resting in the promise without fulfilling the commission?

> **JESUS SHARES WITH US HIS MISSION OF GLOBAL TAKEOVER AND IS WITH US EACH STEP OF THE WAY.**

—— WE PRAY ——

"Jesus, I accept this mission and devote my life to its fulfillment."

> BUT WHEN THEY ARREST YOU, DO NOT WORRY
> ABOUT WHAT TO SAY OR HOW TO SAY IT.
> AT THAT TIME YOU WILL BE GIVEN WHAT TO SAY,
> FOR IT WILL NOT BE YOU SPEAKING, BUT THE SPIRIT
> OF YOUR FATHER SPEAKING THROUGH YOU.
> [MATTHEW 10:19-20]

A directive beginning with "when they arrest you" is not one we often get to literally follow if we're Christians in the United States. But countless Christians over the centuries have found it imminently relevant, and many around the world still do today. We would be foolish to believe it won't perhaps one day apply to us.

When such threats and opposition do come to us, Jesus promises the Holy Spirit will not only give us peace and courage, but also what to say and how to say it. We supply the mouth and mind, God gives the words. Think about it: When I feel tongue-tied about my faith, can I learn to take a deep breath and rely on God to speak through me?

> **IT TAKES COURAGE, NOT ELOQUENCE, TO SPEAK THE GOOD NEWS OF JESUS. HIS SPIRIT SUPPLIES THE WORDS.**

---WE PRAY---

"God, may I share Your Gospel boldly in my actions and Your inspired words."

THE KINGDOM OF THE WORLD HAS BECOME THE KINGDOM OF OUR LORD AND OF HIS MESSIAH, AND HE WILL REIGN FOR EVER AND EVER.
[REVELATION 11:15]

The Way is leading somewhere. Its destination is our destiny: A day in which everyone who's ever lived is fully aware of Jesus as the Forever King, and we His followers are faithful, happy subjects of His eternal, singular Kingdom. This is where the Revolution is heading.

At the beginning, God saw all He had made and said, "It is good." One day He'll finally be able to say that again. He's been waiting and working for that Day. We join Him in that revolutionary work. He gets the final word. We want to be there to hear it.

May we live every day in light of that Day. Prayerfully ponder: On that Day, will I be a farmer who's labored for a great harvest, or a consumer simply full of bread? Will I be a soldier celebrating a hard-fought victory, or a relieved citizen who's only heard reports from the front?

> **EVERY PARLIAMENT, PRINCE, AND PRESIDENT WILL ONE DAY CEDE THEIR REALMS TO THE KING OF ALL KINGDOMS.**

---WE PRAY---

"My King, make my heart Your home, my mind Your throne, my life Your own."

Hope in the Lord and keep his way.
[Psalm 37:34]

AFTERWORD
CALLING ALL WAYKEEPERS

As I conclude and add these final thoughts, I want to note that I've been far more de-scriptive than pre-scriptive in this book, and that's on purpose. My goal here is to inspire you to keep the Way, not necessarily instruct you on exactly how you should or will. This path has enough mystery and adventure for each of us to spend our lives exploring it, discussing it, sharing what we find, and heartening each other to keep to it.

That said, here are some summary observations which highlight what I hope you'll find are the takeaways of this book:

Waykeepers recognize the heroism of steadiness, service, and sacrifice.

Srdja Popovic, who led the movement that helped remove Slobadan Milosevic from Serbia and teaches others how to influence change and topple dictators around the globe, observes: "Proper revolutions are not cataclysmic explosions. They are long, controlled burns."[1] Waykeepers instinctively get this. We walk this path putting one foot in front of the other, keeping our eyes clear and looking forward. Eugene Peterson calls it "a long obedience in the same direction."[2] Being steady shouldn't be confused with being slow or safe. It is about being faithful and even tenacious. People persistently pursuing truth and love is what the world most needs. We season our society like salt. Our faith ferments and adds flavor. We illuminate truth to our culture, providing a steady, warm glow of genuine enlightenment.

Waykeepers take ethics seriously while realizing we don't have it all together.

We comprehend perhaps better than most just how clueless and hopeless we humans are when we live neglecting this Way. "My way doesn't work," we have no trouble admitting. Sure, that sounds humble, but it's also just honest. We know "our way" is another term for sin, which is Scripture's term for what separates us from God and saps our very life. There is no keeping to the Way that doesn't take sin seriously. We do the work of self-reflection that leads to self-awareness. We rejoice to be on "the Way of Holiness." (Isaiah 35:8) Jesus said "only a few find it." (Matthew 7:14) We're so very, very glad we have, and delight in gently guiding others to it. Our Resistance means nothing if it doesn't convey this.

Waykeepers love the Church for all the right reasons.

The Church is a worshipful, diverse community of disciples who've come to understand how much they need—and how great it is to love and follow—Jesus. Our local churches are powerful, supernatural, organized organisms where people serve each other and the world. Tied to the ages, a local church's purpose is simple: be a community of people who support each other in their development as disciples of Jesus who are becoming more and more like Him and spreading His love and message around the world. When a church becomes an institution people support from obligation and not a vibrant family united by and moved by love, then it's lost the Way. Remember: Religious institutions are what we build to feel important, the monuments we construct to commemorate the movement of God. I say, stick with the Mover.

Waykeepers fight for meaning.

Dallas Willard has insightfully observed: "Our most serious failure today is the inability to provide effective practical guidance as to how to live the life of Jesus. And I believe that is due to this very real loss of biblical realism for our lives"[3] The realm of the spiritual, of faith, is too easily relegated as impractical and inconsequential in our culture today. The result? Our "reality" is reduced to the mundane. It can be easy to suffer from the inertia of low expectations and pointlessness that seems to surround us. The everyday becomes routine. We work to survive, to get by so we can get through. Life becomes drained of purpose and passion. Waykeepers feel the true weight of our decisions, sense the spiritual import of our outward circumstances, and grasp the inestimable value of each human soul. With eyes of faith we see a world bathed in God and dripping with potential to know and realize His Kingdom come. We cast off this world's heavy blanket of malaise, fight for every inch of meaning, and maintain God's purposes as our compass. This is the essence of our Rebellion.

Waykeepers relentlessly pursue what matters.

To carry the previous point forward, I believe we are beset by a culture that's absolutely drowning because its adherents can't tell the difference between what's significant and what isn't. The level of energy, concern, and sheer mental RAM that's devoted to who won the game or which show to bingewatch would be mostly benign if equal attention were paid to high school dropout rates or the plight of the homeless. What if we celebrated adoptions as we do touchdowns or rooted on foster families the way we do sports teams? What if our international concerns consisted not only of our reaction to terror but also our response to poverty? What if the "personal best" that mattered most had nothing to do which how fast we run a marathon and everything to do with how well we parent our children or love our spouse? Waykeepers seek to cut through the clamor, invest in what lasts, and accomplish real things. We've realized the broad road to destruction is paved with distraction.

Waykeepers know we're united with all Christians past, present, near and far.

We can't—and don't—go it alone. Not only are we "surrounded by a great cloud of witnesses" (Hebrews 12:1), we are connected to a great movement of Christ-followers around the world. We celebrate and enjoy our diversity. And no matter what we endure, we make sure we don't forget or neglect our kinship to believers suffering persecution, "because [we] know that the family of believers throughout the world is undergoing the same kind of sufferings." (1 Peter 5:9) Many times, they suffer much worse than we. In a very real way, this is the mainspring of our Resistance: "In your struggle against sin, you have not yet resisted to the point of shedding your blood." (Hebrews 12:4)

Waykeepers understand there is no traction without friction.

American Christians lived for a long time with very little dissonance between the practice of their faith and the prevailing view of the surrounding culture. Those days are over, and that's not a completely bad thing. A lack of persecution and pressure is neither normal nor healthy for our faith. Indeed, it's surreal. A genuine keeping to the Way generates some heat and friction. While Waykeepers never pick a fight, we do prepare ourselves for the inevitable conflicts—internal and external—that come with countering the culture. The terms *resistance*, *rebellion*, and *revolution* may seem dramatic, but that doesn't mean they aren't accurate.

Waykeepers make the Great Commission their true north.

There is no keeping to the Way that doesn't stick closely to the final charge of Jesus to His disciples. Oswald J. Smith, a pivotal missions leader, once said: "Any church that is not seriously involved in helping fulfill the Great Commission has forfeited its biblical right to exist."[4] What's true of the Church corporately applies to each of us individually. Missions is not the ministry-of-choice for a few hyperactive Christians. In some way, at some level, missions—the intentional, strategic, prayerful, and demanding work of bringing the Gospel to every people group on the planet—is the calling of every Christ-follower. This is the driving force of the Revolution.

Waykeepers grasp that what this world needs more than anything is Jesus.

All things social, financial, political, and cultural are ultimately spiritual. We don't put our hope in these systems, parties, and institutions—though we know individuals can serve the greater good through service in such sectors to the degree they are deployed there by Jesus their Lord. We are the ones still "saying that there is another king, Jesus."(Acts 17:6-7 ESV) While cups of cold water are given to the thirsty by many all over the world, we realize it's the ones shared in Jesus' Name that carry special promise—for both the giver and the receiver. In other words, we work to do all the good we can, recognizing that humanity's most pressing needs, thorniest problems, and deepest hurts are spiritual and can only truly and fully be met, solved, and healed by Jesus.

Waykeepers make the choice to follow today and every single day.

The writer of Psalm 119:30 declared, "I have chosen the way of faithfulness; I have set my heart on your laws." In his commentary on this verse, Charles Spurgeon made this insightful point: "Men do not drop into the right way by chance; they must choose it, and continue to choose it, or they will soon wander from it." Waykeepers get this, know it in their bones, understand it about themselves. We are humbly aware that we are fully capable of making choices that—while never beyond grace—can do great harm or bring great hurt to ourselves, to our loved ones, as well as to our Lord and His cause. So Spurgeon concludes:

> There is a practical way of truth, the way of holiness, to which we must adhere whatever may be our temptation to forsake it. ...Let us answer to all seducers, "I have chosen, and what I have chosen I have chosen." O Lord, by thy grace lead us with a hearty free-will to choose to do thy will.[5]

Proverbs says it twice to make sure we don't miss it: "There is a way that appears to be right, but in the end it leads to death." (14:12 and 16:25) Thank God there is another Way. We've found Him and been found by Him. We know this Way and get to share it.

I want to keep it and keep to it every day. I'm guessing you do too.

The world needs Waykeepers. So keep your hands to the plow and your eyes on the prize, keep your head clear and right and your heart clean and light, keep your spirits up, and keep up the good work. And above all: Keep to the Way. So much depends on it.

It is God who arms me with strength
and keeps my way secure.
[2 Samuel 22:33 and Psalm 18:32]

Acknowledgements

I'd like to thank my tireless and dedicated ministry assistant, Kim Kiphart, for the research that provides raw material for my sermons, including the ones on which this book is built. I deeply appreciate her hard work and acumen.

Again, I want to express my gratitude for the amalgamation of Waykeepers that is Outlook Christian Church. I'm happy to be a member of our Kingdom community, and especially blessed they allow me to serve them.

I'm so thankful God gave to me my parents, Dale and Christy. Any vision of steadiness and faithfulness I've developed or sought to convey was first firmly planted in me by the two of them. They are for me the very picture and embodiment of these virtues.

I've dedicated this book to my children, Elijah and Hope. At this writing, I'm enjoying the wonder of watching them flourish into young adulthood. Being their father is my highest earthly privilege and calling. No prayer ever crosses my mind or lips more fervently than the one I constantly pray: "May they keep to the Way and become all You, our Father, designed them to be."

As my final word, I give praise to the One who is the Way. "I thank Christ Jesus our Lord, who has given me strength, that he considered me trustworthy, appointing me to his service." (1 Timothy 1:12)

Endnotes

Preface

1. Dallas Willard, *The Spirit of the Disciplines* (New York: HarperCollins Publishers, 1988), Kindle edition, 182.

1 Be the Change

1. Dan Wooding , "The day Mother Teresa told me, 'Your poverty is greater than ours,'" *My Christian Daily*, March 17, 2016, http://www.mychristiandaily.com.au/dr/the-day-mother-teresa-told-me-your-poverty-is-greater-than-ours.
2. Lucinda Vardey, *A Simple Path* (New York: Ballentine Books, 2007).
3. Dietrich Bonhoeffer, *Letters and Papers from Prison* (New York: Touchstone, 1971).

2 Walk the Line

1. I can't put my finger on where I first found the great story behind this song, but you can read more about it here: http://experimentaltheology.blogspot.com/2014/02/the-theology-of-johnny-cash-part-1-i.html.
2. I do not know from which of Goethe's writings this sentence comes, but it is attributed to him by multiple reliable authors across recent decades.
3. David Brooks, *The Road to Character* (New York: Random House, 2015), Kindle edition, location 260.
4. Brooks, *The Road to Character*, location 264.
5. C.S. Lewis, *Mere Christianity* (New York: Touchstone, 1980), 117.
6. A.W. Tozer, *I Call It Heresy* (Harrisburg, Penn: Christian Publications, 1974), 5.
7. Dallas Willard, *The Great Omission* (New York: HarperCollins Publishers, 2006), 34, 62.

3 Always Move Forward

1. C.S. Lewis, *Yours, Jack: Spiritual Direction from C.S. Lewis* (New York: HarperCollins, 2008), Paul Ford, ed., 347.

2. You can catch the whole TED Talk at https://www.ted.com/talks/dan_ariely_on_our_buggy_moral_code/transcript?language=en.
3. Chuck Swindoll, *Come Before Winter and Share My Hope* (Wheaton: Tyndale House, 1985), 202.
4. John R.W. Stott, *Basic Christianity* (London: Inter-Varsity Press, 1999). 108.

4 Stay in the Fight

1. Irenaeus, *Against Heresies, Book 1, Preface*, http://www.ccel.org/ccel/schaff/anf01.ix.ii.i.html.
2. Kristi Burton Brown, "Modern Christians and the Dumbing Down of Sin," *The Christian Post*, July 7, 2015, http://www.christianpost.com/news/modern-christians-and-the-dumbing-down-of-sin-141234/.
3. Louis C.K., *Live at the Beacon Theater* [film] (New York: FX, December 10, 2011).
4. Martin Luther King Jr., *Strength to Love* (Minneapolis: Fortress Press, 2010), 2-3.
5. Jonathan Haidt and Greg Lukianoff, "The Coddling of the American Mind," *The Atlantic*, September 2015, http://www.theatlantic.com/magazine/archive/2015/09/the-coddling-of-the-american-mind/399356/.
6. Lewis, *Mere Christianity*, 51.

5 Control Yourself

1. Leo Tolstoy, "Three Methods Of Reform," *Pamphlets*, 1900, Aylmer Maude, trans., 29.
2. Dallas Willard, *Revolution of Character* (Colorado Springs: NavPress, 2005), 131-132.
3. Beth Moore, *Living Beyond Yourself* (Nashville: LifeWay Press, 2004), 199, 201.
4. This statement is very widely attributed to Mr. Barclay, though I cannot find exactly from which of his works it comes.
5. Brooks, *The Road to Character*, location 245.
6. Brooks, *The Road to Character*, location 248.
7. Timothy Keller, *The Reason for God* (New York: Penguin Group, 2008), Kindle edition, location 1237.
8. Dallas Willard, *Renovation of the Heart* (Colorado Springs: NavPress, 2002), Kindle edition, location 3343.

6 Defy Expectations

1. Billy Graham, "Billy Graham on Being a Nonconformist," Decision Magazine, April 29, 2014, https://billygraham.org/decision-magazine/may-2014/be-a-non-conformist/.
2. You can find the full report here: http://www.pewresearch.org/fact-tank/2015/05/13/a-closer-look-at-americas-rapidly-growing-religious-nones/.
3. Adam Ford, http://adam4d.com/death-of-christianity/.
4. Willard, *The Great Omission*, xv.
5. Hannah More, *The Works of Hannah More, Volume 2* (New York: Harper & Brothers, 1841), 577.
6. Thomas Chalmers, *The Expulsive Power of a New Affection*, cited by Matt Chandler, Eric Geiger, and Josh Patterson in chapter eight of *Creature of the Word* as paraphrased by Chris Farley in *Gospel Powered Parenting*, 24.
7. Beth Moore, *Portraits of Devotion* (Nashville: B&H Publishing, 2014), 12.

8. *Collins English Dictionary—Complete & Unabridged* 10th Edition. HarperCollins Publishers., and *The American Heritage Science Dictionary*. Houghton Mifflin Company.
9. G.K. Chesterton, *The Illustrated London News*, April 19, 1930.
10. G.K. Chesterton, *The Everlasting Man* (Sublime Books, 2014, orig. 1925), Kindle edition, location 3834.
11. Joseph Hoyt, Sarah Kaplan, and Eli Saslow, "Oregon shooter said to have singled out Christians for killing in 'horrific act of cowardice,'" *The Washington Post*, October 2, 2015, https://www.washingtonpost.com/news/morning-mix/wp/2015/10/02/oregon-shooter-said-to-have-singled-out-christians-for-killing-in-horrific-act-of-cowardice/ and "Oregon college shooting: Gunman 'targeted Christians,'" *BBC News*, October 2, 2015, http://www.bbc.com/news/world-us-canada-34424713.

7 Focus on Forever

1. Katie Davis, *Kisses from Katie: A Story of Relentless Love and Redemption* (New York: Howard Books, 2011), 23-24.
2. C.S. Lewis, *The Problem of Pain* (New York: Touchstone, 1996), 103.
3. Tom Sine in *Christianity Today*, March 1989, 52.
4. Hilary Davidson and Christian Smith, *The Paradox of Generosity: Giving We Receive, Grasping We Lose* (New York: Oxford University Press, 2014), 333.
5. A.W. Tozer, *The Pursuit of God* (Camp Hill, Penn: Christian Publications, 1982), 23.
6. C.S. Lewis, *The Screwtape Letters* (New York: Touchstone, 1996), 101.
7. Sine, same as note 3.

8 Belong Together

1. Read about this and more here: http://www.opendoorsusa.org/christian-persecution/.
2. Enjoy a compilation of the Fonz's struggle here: http://www.dailymotion.com/video/x26yzgd_words-fonz-cant-say_fun.
3. Quoted in James E. McGoldrick, *God's Renaissance Man: Abraham Kuyper* (Evangelical Press, 2000), 39.
4. Dietrich Bonhoeffer, *The Cost of Discipleship*, R.H. Fuller, trans. (New York: Macmillan Publishing, 1963), 239.
5. Dietrich Bonhoeffer, *Life Together*, John W. Doberstein, trans. (New York: Harper and Row, 1954), 107.
6. Charles Duhigg, *The Power of Habit* (New York: Random House, 2012), Kindle edition, location 1598.

9 Know Better

1. G.K. Chesterton, *Orthodoxy* (public domain), Kindle edition, locations 21, 27.
2. John Dickson, *A Doubter's Guide to the Ten Commandments* (Grand Rapids: Zondervan, 2016), Kindle edition, location 88.
3. This notion was most recently popularized by *The Wisdom of Crowds: Why the Many Are Smarter Than the Few and How Collective Wisdom Shapes Business, Economies, Societies and Nations*, a book written by James Surowiecki and published in 2004. Learn more at https://en.wikipedia.org/wiki/The_Wisdom_of_Crowds.
4. Dallas Willard, *Hearing God* (Downers Grove: InterVarsity Press, 2012), Kindle edition, location 4827.

5. D.L. Moody quoted in Josiah Hotchkiss Gilbert, *Dictionary of Burning Words of Brilliant Writers* (1895), 622. https://en.wikiquote.org/wiki/Worldliness.
6. Susanna Wesley in a letter to John Wesley, June 8, 1725, quoted in *Susanna Wesley: The Complete Writings*, Charles Wallace Jr., edit. (New York: Oxford University Press, 1997), 109.
7. G.K. Chesterton, *What's Wrong with the World*, Part One, https://www.ccel.org/ccel/chesterton/whatwrong.i.ii.v.html.
8. Mike Erre, *The Jesus of Suburbia: Have we tamed the Son of God to fit our lifestyle?* (Nashville: Thomas Nelson, 2006), 21-22.

10 Light Up the Place

1. Vince Antonucci, *Guerrilla Lovers* (Grand Rapids: Baker Books, 2010), 36.
2. Shane Claiborne, "The Marketable Revolution," *The Simple Way Newsletter*, March 2006, quoted by Tom Sine, *The New Conspirators* (Downers Grove: IVP Books, 2008), 23.
3. It seems to be universally understood that Moody expressed this, but no one I've found states when or where.
4. Willard, *Revolution of Character*, 13-14.
5. As quoted by Bishop Richard Chartres in his sermon to the Royal Wedding congregation at Westminster Abbey (29 April 2011).
6. This story is told in Eusebius' *Ecclesiastical History* VII.22. I first read it in Vince Antonucci's *Guerrilla Lovers*.
7. Brennan Manning, "The Dick Staub Interview: Brennan Manning on Ruthless Trust," *ChristianityToday.com*, December 10, 2002.

11 Send a Message

1. *The Didache* can be read here: http://www.ccel.org/ccel/richardson/fathers.viii.i.iii.html.
2. Mother Teresa, *Jesus is My All in All: Praying with the "Saint of Calcutta"*, Brian Kolodiejchuk, ed (New York: Doubleday, 2008), 41.
3. Charles H. Spurgeon, *Spurgeon At His Best*, compiled by Tom Carter, (Grand Rapids: Baker, 1991), 67.
4. You can catch this video at https://www.buzzfeed.com/kelseypjones/things-christians-want-you-to-know?utm_term=.ewDoo1R83K#.thvyy16m4w.
5. Willard, *The Spirit of the Disciplines*, location 139.

12 Exclude No One

1. Vince Antonucci, *God for the Rest of Us*, (Carol Stream: Tyndale House Publishers, 2015), Kindle edition, location 2817.
2. I cannot recommend the second of these books more highly, *Christ the Lord: The Road to Cana*, especially the audiobook.
3. Sarah Pulliam Bailey, "Q&A: Anne Rice on Following Christ Without Christianity," *Christianity Today*, August 17, 2010, http://www.christianitytoday.com/ct/2010/augustweb-only/43-21.0.html.
4. This statement is consistently attributed to Orwell, but nowhere is it accurately cited. Regardless of who said it, it's true and getting truer.
5. Timothy Keller, *The Meaning of Marriage* (New York: Penguin Group, 2011), 48.
6. Maria Skobtsova, *Mother Maria Skobtsova: Essential Writings*, trans. Richard Pevear and Larissa Volokhonsky (Maryknoll, NY: Orbis Books, 2003), 57.

7. Vince Antonucci conveys this true story powerfully in *God for the Rest of Us*, location 2720, and notes the following: http://www.priestsforlife.org/brochures/whowasthejaneroe.htm, and http://en.wikipedia.org/wiki/Flip_Benham, and http://www.operationsaveamerica.org/misc/misc/aboutUs.html, and http://www.youtube.com/watch?v=tOcRxz3PT6Q.

13 GO AHEAD

1. You can read *The Epistle to Diognetus* at https://www.ccel.org/ccel/richardson/fathers.x.i.ii.html.
2. A.B. Simpson wrote at least thirty books; I do not know in which one he wrote this oft-quoted declaration.
3. Rukmini Callimachi, "ISIS Enshrines a Theology of Rape," *The New York Times*, August 13, 2015, http://www.nytimes.com/2015/08/14/world/middleeast/isis-enshrines-a-theology-of-rape.html?_r=0.
4. You can read Dr. King's entire revolutionary missive here: http://www.thekingcenter.org/archive/document/letter-birmingham-city-jail-0#.
5. Willard, *Revolution of Character*, 13.
6. Os Guinness, *Impossible People: Christian Courage and the Struggle for the Soul of Civilization* (Downers Grove: InterVarsity Press, 2016), Kindle edition, location 918.

AFTERWORD

1. Quoted in Adam Grant, *Originals: How Non-Conformists Move the World* (New York: Viking, 2016), 219-220. Hear more from Popovic at https://www.ted.com/talks/srdja_popovic_how_to_topple_a_dictator.
2. The title of his excellent book: Eugene Peterson, *A Long Obedience in the Same Direction: Discipleship in an Instant Society* (Downers Grove: InterVarsity Press, 2000).
3. Willard, *The Spirit of the Disciplines*, location 2213.
4. Oswald J. Smith (1889-1986) was a Canadian pastor, author, and missions advocate. He preached more than 12,000 sermons in 80 countries, wrote thirty-five books (with translations into 128 languages), as well as 1,200 poems, of which 100 have been set to music. I don't know from which of these this powerful quote comes. Learn more about Smith at https://en.wikipedia.org/wiki/Oswald_J._Smith.
5. C. H. Spurgeon, *The Treasury of David, Volume VI* (New York: Funk & Wagnalls, 1882), 72.

www.ingramcontent.com/pod-product-compliance
Lightning Source LLC
Chambersburg PA
CBHW020743100426
42735CB00037B/290